List Of Contents

Introduction

Welcome to "How To Be Best Friends With Money: The Untold Secret to Making Money Attracted and Stay Beside You." Congratulations on taking the first step towards a life of financial abundance and prosperity. In this book, we'll delve into the transformative power of mindset, exploring the secrets that can attract money into your life, making it a loyal companion on your journey.

The Inspiration Behind the Book

You might wonder what prompted the creation of this book and why it is different from other finance or self-help books out there. The inspiration for "How To Be Best Friends With Money" came from a realization that money, much like a close friend, can influence every aspect of our lives. It can either be a supportive ally or a distant acquaintance, depending on our attitude and approach.

Many of us have experienced moments when money seemed elusive, and no matter how hard we worked, it slipped through our fingers like grains of sand. We wondered why it came effortlessly to some, while we struggled to make ends meet. However, the turning point came when we discovered the profound impact of our thoughts and beliefs on our financial reality.

Our journey to understand the secrets of attracting and retaining money became a quest to discover the untold truth that many successful people seem to know intuitively. We interviewed self-made millionaires, successful entrepreneurs, and individuals who seemed to have a natural affinity for wealth. Their stories were not just about financial strategies, but also about mindset shifts that completely transformed their relationship with money.

The Power of Mindset

As we dived deeper into the subject, we found that the power of mindset was the common thread connecting all these stories. Our thoughts, beliefs, and emotions directly influence the opportunities and possibilities that come our way. In essence, our inner world shapes our outer reality.

This book is not a get-rich-quick scheme or a magic formula to amass wealth overnight. Instead, it's a guide to help you uncover your hidden beliefs about money, and how to shift them to create lasting change. We'll explore the concept of the Law of Attraction, which states that like attracts like. By aligning your thoughts and emotions with abundance, you can draw wealth into your life.

The Abundance Mindset

One of the core principles we'll explore is the abundance mindset. This mindset is a perspective that believes there is enough for everyone and that opportunities are boundless. It contrasts with the scarcity mindset, which fixates on lack and limitation. By cultivating the abundance mindset, you can release fear and worry around money, allowing it to flow freely into your life.

Throughout this book, we'll delve into various techniques and practices to help you embrace the abundance mindset fully. From gratitude rituals to visualization exercises, we'll provide actionable steps that can become a part of your daily routine. The goal is to create lasting change that extends beyond your bank balance and permeates every aspect of your life.

The Magic of Giving

In our pursuit of financial success, we'll also explore the profound impact of giving back. Generosity is not just about financial donations; it's about creating a flow of energy that comes full circle. When you give with a genuine heart, you open up channels for abundance to come back to you in unexpected ways.

A Journey of Growth

As you embark on this journey of embracing abundance, it's essential to remember that growth is a process. Just as you wouldn't expect to become best friends with someone overnight, developing a deep and harmonious relationship with money requires patience and commitment.

Along the way, you'll likely face challenges and obstacles, but these moments present valuable opportunities for growth. We'll explore how to overcome common money fears and navigate through financial setbacks with resilience. Remember that setbacks do not define you; rather, they offer lessons that can guide you toward even greater prosperity.

Your Unique Path to Abundance

As you read through this book, keep in mind that your journey to abundance is unique. What works for one person might not work the same way for another. Embrace the practices and principles that resonate with you, and adapt them to suit your individual circumstances.

This book is not a rigid set of rules but a flexible framework that you can mold to fit your life. It's an invitation to explore new perspectives, challenge old beliefs, and step into the limitless possibilities that await you.

Let's Get Started

So, are you ready to embark on this transformative journey? Together, we'll uncover the untold secrets of attracting money and making it your best friend. By the end of this book, we hope you'll see money in a new light – not as an elusive acquaintance but as a faithful companion that stays beside you on your path to financial abundance.

Let's dive in and discover the magic of embracing abundance, attracting wealth, and making money your best friend!

Chapter 1: Introduction to the Money Mindset

The Power of Mindset in Attracting Money

Welcome to the exciting journey of unlocking the secrets to attracting money and cultivating a prosperous life! In this chapter, we will explore the fundamental role of mindset in shaping your financial reality. You'll discover how the law of attraction plays a crucial role in attracting money and learn techniques to identify and transform limiting beliefs into an abundance mindset.

Understanding the Law of Attraction and Money

Have you ever wondered why some people seem to effortlessly attract wealth and abundance into their lives while others struggle to make ends meet? The answer lies in the powerful principle known as the law of attraction. Simply put, the law of attraction states that like attracts like. In the context of money, this means that your thoughts, beliefs, and emotions about money send out energetic vibrations that resonate with corresponding financial opportunities or lack thereof.

Imagine your mind as a magnet, constantly sending out signals to the universe. If you emit positive thoughts and emotions related to money, you will draw positive financial experiences into your life. Conversely, negative thoughts and emotions can repel money and create financial difficulties. To harness the law of attraction for financial abundance, it's essential to cultivate a positive and abundant money mindset.

Identifying and Changing Limiting Beliefs About Money
Before you can embrace an abundance mindset, it's crucial to identify and address any limiting beliefs you may have about money. Limiting beliefs are deep-seated thoughts and attitudes that create barriers to financial success. They often stem from childhood experiences, cultural influences, or negative past experiences with money.

Common limiting beliefs about money include:

- "Money is the root of all evil."

- "I'll never be wealthy; it's just not in my cards."

- "I'm not good with money; I can never manage it well."

- "Rich people are greedy and selfish."

These beliefs act as self-fulfilling prophecies, subconsciously influencing your financial decisions and actions. The good news is that beliefs are not fixed; they can be changed with conscious effort and repetition.

To transform limiting beliefs about money:

1. Recognize and Acknowledge: Begin by acknowledging your limiting beliefs. Awareness is the first step in overcoming them.

2. Challenge the Belief: Question the validity of the belief. Is it based on facts or assumptions? Often, limiting beliefs are irrational and unfounded.

3. Replace with Empowering Beliefs: Replace limiting beliefs with positive, empowering statements. For example, "I am capable of managing money wisely and attracting abundance."

4. Reinforce Daily: Repetition is key to reinforcing new beliefs. Create affirmations and repeat them daily to rewire your subconscious mind.

5. Visualize the Desired Outcome: Visualize yourself living with financial abundance. Feel the emotions associated with having an abundance of money.

Embracing an Abundance Mindset
Now that you've begun the process of transforming limiting beliefs, it's time to embrace an abundance mindset fully. An abundance mindset is a state of mind where you believe that there are abundant opportunities for wealth and prosperity available to you and others.

Embracing an abundance mindset practice:

1. Gratitude and Positivity: Practice gratitude for the money you have and the opportunities that come your way. Focus on positive aspects of your financial journey.

2. Focus on Possibilities: Instead of dwelling on lack or scarcity, direct your focus toward potential opportunities and possibilities to create wealth.

3. Take Inspired Action: Combine positive thinking with purposeful action. Take steps towards your financial goals with enthusiasm and confidence.

4. Celebrate Abundance Around You: Celebrate the success and abundance of others, as it reinforces your belief that abundance is possible for everyone.

5. Trust the Process: Have faith in the universe's ability to support your financial desires. Trust that your positive mindset will attract the right circumstances.

Remember, embracing an abundance mindset is not about denying financial challenges or ignoring practical responsibilities. Instead, it's about creating a positive and empowered relationship with money, which sets the foundation for attracting and manifesting financial abundance into your life.

As you continue your journey into the world of money mindset, always remember that changing your thoughts and beliefs is a gradual process. Be patient with yourself, stay committed to growth, and watch how the power of mindset transforms your financial reality for the better. Embrace the journey and get ready for an abundance of opportunities and prosperity coming your way!

Rewiring Your Brain for Wealth

In this section, we will explore the fascinating world of neuroplasticity and how you can use it to rewire your brain for financial abundance. Get ready to unleash the power of your mind as we delve into the essential techniques of affirmations, visualization, and creating a positive money script that will set you on the path to manifesting money effortlessly.

The Role of Neuroplasticity in Shaping Money Habits

Did you know that your brain is a highly adaptable organ that can be rewired and reshaped throughout your life? This phenomenon is known as neuroplasticity, and it's the key to changing your money habits and mindset. Our brains are wired to follow well-established neural pathways, which influence our thoughts, emotions, and behaviors around money. But the good news is that we can actively create new neural pathways to replace old, limiting beliefs about money.

Neuroplasticity works on the principle of "use it or lose it." When you consistently reinforce positive money habits and thoughts, the neural connections associated with those habits become stronger. On the other hand, if you continually dwell on negative thoughts about money, those connections remain dominant. By understanding this concept, you can begin to reshape your relationship with money by consciously directing your thoughts and actions.

To start rewiring your brain for wealth, begin by identifying any limiting beliefs you have about money.

These might include thoughts like "money is scarce," "I'll never be wealthy," or "rich people are greedy." Once you've identified these beliefs, challenge them with evidence to the contrary. Seek out examples of people who have achieved financial success through ethical means and who use their wealth to make a positive impact in the world. This process will help weaken the neural pathways associated with limiting beliefs.

Using Affirmations and Visualization to Manifest Money
Affirmations are powerful tools to help rewire your brain for wealth. These are positive, present-tense statements that affirm the reality you want to create. For example, you might say, "I am a money magnet," "Money flows to me effortlessly," or "I attract abundance in all areas of my life." By repeating these affirmations daily, you send positive messages to your subconscious mind, gradually replacing old negative thought patterns with new, empowering ones.

Visualization is another technique to complement affirmations. Take a few minutes each day to close your eyes and vividly imagine yourself living the life of financial abundance you desire. Visualize the lifestyle, experiences, and opportunities that come with having an abundance of money. Engage all your senses in this visualization, and feel the emotions associated with financial prosperity. When you consistently visualize this reality, you align your subconscious mind with your conscious goals, making them more attainable.

Creating a Positive Money Script

A money script is the internal dialogue we have with ourselves about money, often formed during childhood based on our upbringing, experiences, and societal influences. These scripts can be positive or negative and significantly impact our financial behaviors. To manifest money effortlessly, it's crucial to create a positive money script that supports your goals and aspirations.

Start by observing your current money script. Are there recurring negative thoughts or self-doubts about money? Write them down and then challenge them one by one. Replace these negative statements with positive affirmations that reflect your financial goals and values.

For example, if your old money script says, "I will never be able to save enough money," change it to "I am capable of managing my finances wisely, and I save effortlessly." By consistently reinforcing this positive script, you'll begin to internalize it, and it will guide your financial decisions in alignment with your goals.

Rewiring your brain for wealth is an ongoing process. Be patient with yourself and practice self-compassion as you work to change old money habits and beliefs. Celebrate every small step towards progress, as each one brings you closer to the abundant life you desire.

The power of neuroplasticity, affirmations, visualization, and a positive money script can profoundly influence your financial journey. Embrace these techniques and make them a part of your daily routine. By rewiring your brain for wealth, you'll open the doors to unlimited possibilities and attract money effortlessly, allowing abundance to flow into every aspect of your life. Get ready to experience the transformative magic of your money mindset!

Cultivating Gratitude and Abundance

In our quest for financial abundance, we often seek external solutions, believing that money will flow into our lives through hard work and luck alone. However, what many of us fail to realize is that the key to unlocking the door to prosperity lies within us. The way we think, feel, and interact with money has a significant impact on how it shows up in our lives. In this section, we will explore the profound connection between gratitude and money, and how cultivating a mindset of abundance can attract financial prosperity into our lives.

The Gratitude-Money Connection

Gratitude is a powerful and transformative emotion that can shape our relationship with money. When we approach our financial situation with a sense of gratitude, we shift our focus from what we lack to what we already have. This shift in perspective is crucial because it allows us to acknowledge and appreciate the abundance that already exists in our lives.

Expressing gratitude for the money we currently have opens the doors to receiving more. Gratitude operates on the principle of the law of attraction, which suggests that like attracts like. When we emanate positive energy through gratitude, we become a magnet for more positive experiences, including financial abundance.

It's essential to avoid falling into the trap of constant comparison with others. Social media and society often make it easy for us to feel inadequate about our financial status. However, when we redirect our focus to the things we are grateful for, we can break free from the scarcity mindset and embrace abundance.

Practicing Daily Gratitude for Financial Abundance
To harness the power of gratitude, it is crucial to make it a daily practice. Incorporating gratitude into your daily routine can be as simple as setting aside a few minutes each morning or evening to reflect on the blessings in your life.

One effective practice is to keep a gratitude journal. Take a few moments each day to write down three to five things you are thankful for regarding your financial situation. These can range from having a stable job, meeting your basic needs, or even small moments of unexpected financial blessings. The act of writing down your blessings helps anchor them in your consciousness and amplifies their positive impact on your life.

Another powerful way to practice gratitude is through visualization. Take some time each day to close your eyes

and envision your financial goals as if they have already
come to fruition. Feel the emotions of gratitude and joy as
you experience the fulfillment of your financial desires.
Visualization helps align your subconscious mind with
your financial goals, making it easier to attract them into
your reality.

Abundance Rituals and Practices
In addition to daily gratitude practices, incorporating
abundance rituals into your life can significantly impact
your financial mindset. Abundance rituals are symbolic acts
that represent your intention to attract financial prosperity.
These rituals help create a positive energy flow and align
your actions with your financial desires.

One popular abundance ritual is creating a vision board.
Gather images and words that represent your financial
goals and aspirations, such as a dream house, a vacation
destination, or a successful business venture. Place these
images on a board and display it prominently in your living
space. The vision board serves as a constant reminder of
your financial vision and keeps you motivated to achieve
your goals.

Another powerful abundance ritual is the act of giving
back. When we share our blessings with others through
charitable acts, donations, or volunteering, we send a clear
message to the universe that we trust in the flow of
abundance. Giving back creates a sense of fulfillment and
satisfaction, reinforcing the belief that we have more than
enough to share.

Furthermore, mindfulness practices such as meditation and deep breathing can also help cultivate abundance. By grounding ourselves in the present moment, we release worries about the past or future and open ourselves up to the abundance available in the here and now.

Cultivating gratitude and abundance is a transformative practice that can revolutionize our financial lives. By shifting our perspective from scarcity to sufficiency, we become magnets for financial prosperity. Daily gratitude practices and abundance rituals not only help us attract more money but also lead to a more fulfilling and purposeful life. As you embark on this journey of embracing the money mindset, remember that the true essence of abundance lies not only in material wealth but also in the richness of our thoughts, emotions, and connections with others.

Chapter 2: Setting Clear Financial Goals

The Importance of Goal Setting for Financial Success

Hey there, future financial trailblazer! Welcome to Chapter 2 of our journey toward attracting and sustaining abundant wealth. In this section, we're going to delve into the heart of financial success – goal setting! Setting clear financial goals is like drawing a roadmap to your dream life, guiding you through the twists and turns of your financial journey. Are you ready to take control of your financial destiny? Let's dive in!

The Power of Goal Setting

Picture this: you embark on a road trip without a destination in mind. While the idea of a spontaneous adventure might sound exciting, you'll likely end up lost and confused, wandering aimlessly. The same principle applies to your financial journey. Setting clear goals acts as your destination, providing focus, direction, and motivation.

Setting Specific and Realistic Financial Goals

The key to effective goal setting is to make your objectives specific and realistic. Vague or overly ambitious goals can lead to frustration and demotivation. Start by identifying precisely what you want to achieve. Is it buying a new home, paying off debts, or funding a dream vacation?

Once you have your goals in mind, put some numbers to them. Define the amount of money you need to achieve each goal and set a realistic timeframe. Break larger goals into smaller, manageable milestones, making your progress more tangible and achievable.

For example, if you aim to save $10,000 for an emergency fund in one year, you can set monthly savings targets of around $833. This specific and realistic approach will boost your confidence and keep you on track.

Creating a Vision Board for Financial Dreams
Now that you've set your financial goals, it's time to add a touch of creativity to the process. Vision boards are powerful visual tools that help manifest your dreams into reality. They serve as a collage of images, quotes, and symbols representing your financial aspirations.

Start by gathering magazines, printouts, or even digital images that resonate with your goals. If you want to own a beachfront property, include pictures of your dream house. If you aspire to retire early and travel the world, add images of exotic destinations.

Create your vision board by arranging these elements on a poster board or a digital canvas. Place it somewhere visible, like your bedroom or office, to keep your financial dreams in focus every day. The visualization of your goals will act as a constant reminder and help you stay motivated.

Building a Roadmap to Financial Freedom
With specific goals and a vision board in hand, it's time to construct your roadmap to financial freedom. A financial roadmap outlines the steps and strategies you'll take to achieve your objectives. This plan will serve as your GPS, guiding you through the twists and turns of your financial journey.

Start by assessing your current financial situation. Evaluate your income, expenses, debts, and assets. This analysis will highlight areas that need improvement and opportunities for growth.

Next, craft a budget that aligns with your goals and sets aside funds for saving and investing. Your budget should strike a balance between enjoying the present while securing your financial future.

Consider diversifying your income streams, such as starting a side hustle, investing in stocks, or creating passive income sources. A diversified income will provide stability and accelerate your journey toward financial freedom.

Lastly, don't forget to track your progress regularly. Revisit your financial goals, review your achievements, and make adjustments to your roadmap if necessary. Celebrate every milestone along the way, as each step takes you closer to the ultimate prize – financial abundance.

Congratulations! You've taken a significant step toward achieving financial success by setting clear and realistic goals. Remember, the journey to wealth may have its challenges, but with a well-defined roadmap, you'll navigate through any obstacle that comes your way.

As you move forward, keep your vision board close, visualizing your dreams manifesting into reality. Stay committed to your financial goals, and let your passion for a prosperous life fuel your determination. You have the power to attract money and make your dreams come true. Now, let's continue this journey to discover the untold secrets of financial abundance!

Overcoming Money Blocks and Resistance

Welcome to the second chapter of "How To Be Best Friends With Money: The Untold Secret to Making Money Attracted and Stay Beside You." In this section, we will delve into the crucial aspect of overcoming money blocks and resistance, which can hinder our path to financial success. Many of us face these challenges at some point in our lives, but with the right mindset and strategies, we can break free and stay committed to our financial goals.

Identifying and Addressing Financial Procrastination

Let's face it; procrastination is something we have all experienced in various aspects of our lives. When it comes to money matters, procrastination can be a significant obstacle to achieving our financial goals. It's that little voice in our heads that says, "I'll start saving tomorrow," or "I'll invest when I have more money." Unfortunately, tomorrow often turns into the next day, and the cycle continues.

One of the first steps to overcoming financial procrastination is to recognize it for what it is—a fear-based reaction to uncertainty or discomfort. We might fear making the wrong financial decisions, fear facing our financial reality, or fear that we're not capable of handling our finances effectively. By acknowledging these fears, we can start dismantling the mental barriers holding us back.

To address financial procrastination, consider the following key points:

1. Break Tasks into Smaller Steps: Large financial goals can feel overwhelming, leading to procrastination. Break them down into smaller, manageable tasks. For instance, if your goal is to create an emergency fund, start by saving a small amount each week.

2. Set Realistic Deadlines: Establish deadlines for each financial task to keep yourself accountable. Share your goals with a friend or family member who can provide encouragement and support.

3. Cultivate Self-Compassion: Understand that setbacks happen, and it's okay to make mistakes. Treat yourself with kindness and learn from any financial missteps.

Dealing with Fear of Success and Fear of Failure

Believe it or not, both the fear of success and the fear of failure can prevent us from reaching our financial potential. The fear of success might be rooted in the fear of change or the pressure to sustain success once achieved. On the other hand, the fear of failure often stems from the fear of judgment or the belief that failure defines our worth.

To overcome these fears, let's focus on the following key points:

1. Embrace Growth Mindset: Adopt a growth mindset that views success and failure as opportunities for learning and growth. Celebrate your successes, and view failures as stepping stones toward improvement.

2. Rewrite Your Money Story: Reflect on your beliefs about money and success. Challenge any negative beliefs and replace them with positive, empowering affirmations.

3. Visualize Success: Visualize yourself achieving your financial goals and experiencing the benefits. This can reinforce your commitment and build excitement about your financial journey.

Strategies to Stay Committed to Your Financial Goals

Staying committed to our financial goals requires consistent effort and dedication. Here are some strategies to help you maintain focus and perseverance:

1. Create a Financial Vision Board: Compile images and words that represent your financial goals and aspirations.

Display the vision board where you can see it daily to reinforce your commitment.

2. Track Your Progress: Regularly review your financial progress. Seeing the positive changes over time can be incredibly motivating.

3. Reward Yourself: Celebrate milestones along the way. Rewarding yourself for reaching financial goals will make the journey more enjoyable and fulfilling.

4. Build a Support System: Surround yourself with individuals who share similar financial aspirations. Join financial groups or forums where you can exchange ideas and encouragement.

5. Review and Adjust Goals: Life circumstances can change, and so can your financial goals. Regularly review your objectives and adjust them as needed to stay aligned with your current situation.

Remember, overcoming money blocks and resistance is a process that requires patience and persistence. Be gentle with yourself and celebrate every step you take towards financial empowerment. In the next chapter, we will explore the concept of creating multiple streams of income and investing in yourself to unlock even greater financial abundance.

Keep going, and remember, you have the power to attract and keep money beside you with the right mindset and determination!

The Power of Focus and Persistence

Setting clear financial goals is the first step toward achieving financial success and abundance. However, having goals alone is not enough; you need the power of focus and persistence to turn those dreams into reality. In this section, we'll explore how concentrating your efforts, embracing perseverance, and celebrating milestones and small wins can propel you on the path to financial prosperity.

Concentrating Your Efforts for Maximum Impact

Imagine standing in front of a vast buffet with dozens of delicious dishes. If you try to taste every single item, you'll end up with a full plate, but you won't fully savor the flavors of any particular dish. Similarly, when it comes to your financial goals, trying to pursue too many objectives at once can lead to scattered efforts and lackluster results.

Instead, focus on a few key financial goals that truly resonate with you. Determine what matters most in your life, whether it's paying off debt, saving for a down payment on a home, or building an investment portfolio. Concentrate your energy, time, and resources on achieving those specific objectives. By channeling your efforts toward a select few goals, you'll increase your chances of success and experience a more profound sense of accomplishment.

One effective technique is to prioritize your goals using the "SMART" criteria:

- **Specific**: Make your goals clear and well-defined.

- **Measurable**: Set quantifiable targets to track your progress.

- **Achievable**: Ensure your goals are realistic and within reach.

- **Relevant**: Align your objectives with your values and long-term vision.

- **Time-bound**: Set a deadline for achieving each goal to maintain focus.

Remember, focus doesn't mean you can't pursue other goals later; it's about directing your energy efficiently for maximum impact.

Embracing Perseverance in the Face of Challenges
Life rarely unfolds without challenges, and your financial journey is no exception. You might encounter unexpected setbacks, face financial roadblocks, or even experience moments of doubt. During these times, embracing perseverance is crucial to staying on track and overcoming obstacles.

Perseverance is the determination to keep going, even when the going gets tough. It means staying committed to your financial goals despite setbacks and failures. Understand that setbacks are a natural part of any journey, and they provide valuable opportunities for growth and learning.

Celebrating Milestones and Small Wins

As you progress on your financial journey, it's essential to celebrate the milestones and small wins you achieve along the way. Celebrations not only provide positive reinforcement but also serve as a reminder of the progress you've made.

Recognize that financial success is not a one-time event; it's a series of achievements, both big and small. Each step forward is worth acknowledging. Whether it's paying off a credit card, reaching a savings milestone, or securing a new income stream, take the time to celebrate your victories.

Celebrations don't have to be extravagant or expensive. Simple gestures, such as treating yourself to a favorite meal or taking a day off to relax, can be just as rewarding. Additionally, sharing your achievements with loved ones can strengthen your support network and inspire others on their financial journeys.

It's essential to enjoy the ride. Celebrating milestones and small wins will not only motivate you to keep going but also make the process more enjoyable.

The power of focus and persistence can be transformative on your financial journey. By concentrating your efforts on specific goals, embracing perseverance in the face of challenges, and celebrating every milestone, you set yourself up for success. Stay positive, stay determined, and remember that every step you take brings you closer to financial abundance and a brighter future.

Chapter 3: Creating Multiple Streams of Income

Understanding the Concept of Multiple Streams of Income

Hey there, welcome to Chapter 3 of our exciting journey towards becoming best friends with money! In this chapter, we'll dive deep into the concept of creating multiple streams of income. It's like having a bouquet of money flowers coming your way from various sources, ensuring a steady and abundant financial flow. Are you ready to explore the world of income diversification? Let's get started!

Diversifying Your Income Sources

Imagine if all your eggs were in one basket, and that basket suddenly developed a hole – you'd be left with a mess, right? Well, the same principle applies to your finances. Relying solely on a single source of income can be risky, as it leaves you vulnerable to unexpected changes in the job market or economic fluctuations. That's where the beauty of diversification comes into play.

Diversifying your income means having multiple streams that bring money into your life. These streams could come from different sources, such as salary from your primary job, profits from investments, earnings from side hustles, or royalties from creative works. By spreading your financial sources, you're building a safety net that can catch you during uncertain times and propel you towards financial prosperity.

Now, diversifying doesn't mean juggling a dozen part-time jobs simultaneously – it's about finding opportunities that align with your interests, skills, and passions. The goal is to strike a balance between stability and potential growth, all while exploring various income avenues.

Exploring Passive Income Opportunities
Who doesn't love the idea of making money while sipping a coconut on a tropical beach? That's where passive income comes in – it's like having a money tree that bears fruit without you having to toil under the scorching sun.

Passive income refers to money earned with little to no active effort on your part. It's about making smart investments, creating assets, or setting up systems that generate income automatically. Some popular forms of passive income include rental properties, dividend-paying stocks, interest from savings accounts, and income from digital products like e-books or online courses.

One of the advantages of passive income is that it can provide financial stability and free up your time to focus on other ventures or simply enjoy life. Remember, building passive income streams may require initial effort and investment, but the long-term benefits are worth it. So, plant those money trees and let them grow while you live life to the fullest!

Here are some passive income ideas worth exploring:

Rental Properties: Owning real estate and renting it out can be an excellent source of passive income. Whether it's a residential property or a commercial space, rental income can provide a steady cash flow.

Investing in Dividend Stocks: Some companies distribute a portion of their profits to shareholders in the form of dividends. Investing in dividend-paying stocks can provide a reliable stream of passive income.

Affiliate Marketing: If you have a blog or a website with a decent following, you can earn passive income by promoting other people's products or services through affiliate marketing. You earn a commission for every sale made through your referral link.

Leveraging Your Skills and Talents for Extra Income
We all have unique skills and talents that can be transformed into profitable ventures. Whether you're a coding wizard, a master chef, a talented artist, or a gifted writer, there's an opportunity to turn your passion into a side gig that earns you extra cash.

First, identify your strengths and interests. What do you love doing, and what are you naturally good at? Next, think about how you can leverage these skills to provide value to others. For instance, if you're an excellent writer, you could freelance as a content creator. If you're a fitness enthusiast, you might consider becoming a personal trainer on weekends.

With the internet at your fingertips, the possibilities are endless. You can sell your products or services online, offer consulting, or even create a YouTube channel showcasing your expertise. Remember, it's not just about making money; it's about doing what you love and sharing your gifts with the world.

Now that you know the power of multiple income streams, it's time to take action. Start by identifying potential opportunities that align with your interests and strengths. Explore, experiment, and don't be afraid to take calculated risks. Before you know it, you'll be reaping the rewards of your diverse financial endeavors.

Investing in Yourself and Your Financial Education

In this section, we will explore the invaluable concept of investing in yourself and your financial education. The journey to building multiple streams of income begins with a commitment to lifelong learning, a willingness to embrace new knowledge, and an openness to personal growth. So, let's dive in and discover the key aspects of this essential step on your path to financial abundance.

The Importance of Lifelong Learning in Wealth Building
In the fast-paced and ever-changing world we live in,
continuous learning is not just an option; it's a necessity for
personal and financial growth. The most successful
individuals understand that knowledge is power, and it is
the key to unlocking new opportunities and potential
streams of income.

Lifelong learning in the context of wealth building involves
a mindset shift towards seeing every experience as an
opportunity to learn. Whether it's reading books, attending
seminars, taking online courses, or simply staying informed
about industry trends, every piece of knowledge you
acquire can be an asset in your journey towards financial
prosperity.

Moreover, the process of learning itself can lead to
enhanced problem-solving abilities, creativity, and
adaptability—traits that are highly valuable in navigating
the complexities of the financial landscape. Embrace the
idea that you are your greatest asset, and by investing in
your knowledge, you are investing in your future.

Investing in Courses, Workshops, and Seminars
One of the most effective ways to invest in your financial
education is by enrolling in courses, workshops, and
seminars that align with your interests and aspirations.
Thanks to advancements in technology, there are now
countless online platforms and educational institutions
offering a wide array of courses on various subjects,
including finance, entrepreneurship, marketing, and more.

Before diving in, take some time to identify your goals and areas where you'd like to deepen your understanding. Are you interested in exploring real estate investment, stock trading, or digital marketing? Perhaps you're keen on starting a side business or venturing into the world of cryptocurrencies. Whatever your interests, there is likely a course or workshop tailored to meet your needs.

While some courses may come with a price tag, view them as valuable investments rather than expenses. Consider the potential return on investment—how the knowledge gained could lead to new income opportunities or increased efficiency in managing your finances.

Building a Network of Like-Minded Individuals
The saying, "Your network is your net worth," holds true in the world of finance. Surrounding yourself with like-minded individuals who share similar financial goals and aspirations can be a powerful catalyst for success. Networking not only opens doors to new opportunities but also provides valuable insights and support from those who have walked a similar path.

Start by attending industry events, workshops, and conferences related to your areas of interest. Engage with speakers, participants, and organizers, and be open to forming genuine connections. Don't underestimate the power of online communities and social media platforms, where you can find groups of individuals with shared interests.

Through networking, you can learn from others' experiences, gain access to potential business partners or clients, and even discover new investment opportunities. Remember, building a network is not just about what you can gain; it's also about what you can contribute. Be willing to share your knowledge and experiences, as this reciprocity strengthens relationships and fosters a supportive community.

Investing in yourself and your financial education is a crucial step towards creating multiple streams of income. Embrace a growth mindset, seek out opportunities to learn, and connect with like-minded individuals who can inspire and support your journey. Remember, the journey to financial abundance is not a sprint; it's a marathon. So, stay committed, keep learning, and watch as your efforts unfold into a world of new possibilities and prosperity. Happy learning!

Building a Profitable Business or Side Hustle

In today's dynamic economy, relying solely on a single source of income may not provide the financial security and abundance we desire. To truly thrive, it's essential to explore and develop multiple streams of income. One of the most effective ways to achieve this is by starting a profitable business or engaging in a side hustle. In this section, we will explore the key steps to build a successful business or side venture that aligns with your passions and financial goals.

Identifying a Profitable Niche or Business Idea
The foundation of any successful business or side hustle begins with a well-defined and profitable niche. Identifying the right niche is like finding a fertile ground where your ideas can take root and flourish. Here are some essential steps to help you discover a niche that resonates with you:

1. Passion and Purpose: Start by considering your interests, skills, and passions. What activities bring you joy and fulfillment? Combining your passions with your expertise will not only keep you motivated but also set you apart from competitors.

2. Market Research: Conduct thorough market research to understand the demand for products or services in your chosen niche. Analyze the needs and pain points of your target audience and explore how you can offer unique solutions.

3. Competition Analysis: Assess your potential competitors to identify gaps in the market. Look for opportunities to provide something different or better than what is currently available.

4. Scalability and Longevity: Choose a niche that has the potential for growth and sustainability over the long term. Consider trends and emerging markets to ensure your business remains relevant in the future.

Marketing and Promoting Your Business Effectively

Once you've established your niche and business idea, the next step is to effectively market and promote your offerings to your target audience. Marketing is the key to attracting customers and generating revenue. Here are some valuable strategies to help you market your business or side hustle effectively:

1. Build an Online Presence: In today's digital age, having an online presence is crucial. Create a professional website and use social media platforms to reach a broader audience. Engage with potential customers through valuable content and interactions.

2. Content Marketing: Share informative and engaging content related to your niche. This could include blog posts, videos, podcasts, or social media content. Providing value to your audience establishes your authority and builds trust.

3. Networking and Partnerships: Attend industry events, join networking groups, and collaborate with other businesses or influencers in your niche. Building relationships can lead to valuable partnerships and increased exposure for your business.

4. Offer Promotions and Incentives: Attract customers with special offers, discounts, or loyalty programs. This can encourage repeat business and word-of-mouth referrals.

5. Customer Testimonials and Reviews: Encourage satisfied customers to leave testimonials and reviews. Positive feedback builds credibility and can sway potential customers in your favor.

Managing Finances and Scaling Your Business

As your business or side hustle grows, effective financial management becomes essential. Properly managing your finances ensures the sustainability and scalability of your venture. Here are some essential financial practices to implement:

1. Budgeting and Expense Tracking: Create a budget that outlines your income and expenses. Monitor your spending to ensure you are staying within your financial limits.

2. Separate Business and Personal Finances: Open a separate bank account for your business to keep personal and business finances distinct. This simplifies accounting and ensures accurate financial records.

3. Invest in Tools and Technology: Utilize financial software or apps to streamline your financial processes. This can help with invoicing, payment tracking, and financial reporting.

4. Seek Professional Advice: Consult with an accountant or financial advisor to ensure you're making informed decisions. They can provide valuable insights on tax planning, investment strategies, and financial growth.

5. Scale Wisely: As your business grows, evaluate opportunities for expansion carefully. Ensure you have the resources and infrastructure to handle increased demand without compromising quality.

Building a profitable business or side hustle is an empowering journey that offers both financial rewards and personal fulfillment. By identifying a profitable niche, effectively marketing your offerings, and managing your finances wisely, you can create a thriving venture that complements your other income streams. Remember to stay adaptable and open to learning, as entrepreneurship involves continuous growth and evolution. With dedication, passion, and strategic planning, you can transform your business idea into a thriving reality and set yourself on the path to financial abundance.

Chapter 4: Mastering the Art of Budgeting and Saving

The Foundation of Financial Stability: Budgeting

Welcome to Chapter 4 of "How To Be Best Friends With Money." In this section, we'll explore the crucial aspect of financial stability: budgeting. Budgeting is like the blueprint of your financial journey, guiding you towards a life of abundance and prosperity. By creating a personalized budget, tracking your expenses, and avoiding common pitfalls, you'll gain the confidence to take control of your finances and pave the way for a brighter financial future.

Creating a Personalized Budget

Think of a budget as a roadmap to achieving your financial goals. It's a clear, organized plan that reflects your income, expenses, and savings targets. When creating a personalized budget, you'll need to consider your unique financial situation and lifestyle. Here's how to get started:

1. Assess Your Income: Begin by calculating your total monthly income. Include all sources of income, such as your salary, bonuses, freelance work, and any other additional earnings. Knowing your income is essential to make realistic financial decisions.

2. Track Your Expenses: To create an accurate budget, you'll need to track your expenses diligently. Keep a record of every penny you spend for at least a month. Categorize your expenses into fixed (e.g., rent, utilities) and variable (e.g., groceries, entertainment) costs. This will provide insights into where your money is going.

3. Set Financial Goals: Take the time to define your short-term and long-term financial goals. Whether it's saving for an emergency fund, paying off debt, or investing for retirement, knowing your objectives will help you allocate your funds more effectively.

4. Budgeting Tools: Embrace the power of technology by using budgeting apps or spreadsheets to manage your finances. These tools can simplify the budgeting process and offer visual representations of your financial progress.

5. Be Realistic: When creating a budget, be honest with yourself about your spending habits. While it's essential to cut unnecessary expenses, don't set unrealistic targets that may lead to frustration and failure. Be flexible and adjust your budget as needed.

Tracking Expenses and Identifying Saving Opportunities: Once you've established your budget, the next step is tracking your expenses and identifying areas where you can save money. This process can be both enlightening and empowering:

1. Monitor Your Spending: Keep a close eye on your expenses using your budgeting tool or app. Regularly review your spending patterns to ensure you stay on track.

2. Identify Non-Essential Expenses: Look for areas where you can cut back without sacrificing your quality of life.

Perhaps dining out less frequently or reducing impulse purchases can free up more money for savings.

3. Set Savings Targets: Aim to save a certain percentage of your income each month. Financial experts recommend saving at least 20% of your income, but adjust this figure based on your individual goals and circumstances.

4. Automate Savings: Take advantage of automation to make saving effortless. Set up automatic transfers to your savings account or retirement fund as soon as your paycheck arrives. This way, you won't be tempted to spend money earmarked for savings.

Avoiding Common Budgeting Pitfalls

Budgeting isn't always smooth sailing, and it's easy to fall into common traps. Here are some pitfalls to avoid to maintain a successful budget:

1. Neglecting Emergency Fund: Life is full of surprises, and unexpected expenses can quickly derail your budget. Prioritize building an emergency fund to cover unforeseen events, such as medical emergencies or car repairs.

2. Ignoring Irregular Expenses: Many people forget to account for irregular expenses like annual insurance premiums or holiday gifts in their budgets. Create a separate category for these expenses and set aside money each month to avoid last-minute financial stress.

3. Failing to Review and Adjust: A budget is a living document that should adapt to changes in your life.

Regularly review your budget and make adjustments as needed. If you get a raise or experience a decrease in income, adjust your budget accordingly.

4. Succumbing to Lifestyle Inflation: As your income increases, it's tempting to upgrade your lifestyle. However, be mindful of lifestyle inflation, as it can hinder your ability to achieve long-term financial goals.

Be patient with yourself and celebrate your progress, no matter how small. Budgeting is a powerful tool that will pave the way for a stable financial future, bringing you one step closer to attracting and keeping the money you desire in your life.

Building a Strong Saving and Emergency Fund

In this section, we'll delve into the crucial topic of building a strong saving and emergency fund, a cornerstone of financial security and peace of mind. Life is full of uncertainties, and having a safety net can make all the difference during challenging times. So, let's explore the importance of emergency funds, effective strategies for consistent saving and investing, and how to handle unexpected financial challenges.

The Importance of Emergency Funds in Financial Security

Imagine waking up one day to find yourself facing an unexpected car repair bill, a medical emergency, or an unforeseen job loss. Without an emergency fund, these situations can quickly spiral into financial stress and burden. An emergency fund acts as a financial cushion, ready to support you when life throws unexpected curveballs.

But how much should you have in your emergency fund? A common rule of thumb is to aim for three to six months' worth of living expenses. This amount provides a safety net to cover essential costs like housing, utilities, groceries, and transportation, allowing you to focus on finding solutions during difficult times.

Start by analyzing your monthly expenses and set a realistic savings goal. If building a fully-funded emergency fund seems daunting, don't worry. Start small and gradually work your way up. Every contribution matters, and you'll be amazed at how quickly your fund grows with consistent effort.

Strategies for Consistent Saving and Investing

Now that we understand the significance of emergency funds, let's explore some practical strategies for consistent saving and investing. These habits will not only help you build an emergency fund but also pave the way to long-term financial success.

1. Pay Yourself First: Treat your savings as a non-negotiable expense. When you receive your paycheck, allocate a portion of it directly to your savings account before spending on other expenses. This approach ensures that you prioritize your financial well-being.

2. Automate Your Savings: Take advantage of technology by setting up automatic transfers from your checking account to your savings account. Automating your savings makes it easier to stick to your financial goals and reduces the temptation to spend the money elsewhere.

3. Create a Budget: A budget is an indispensable tool for managing your finances effectively. Track your income and expenses, identify areas where you can cut back, and allocate a portion of your income to savings each month.

4. Utilize Windfalls Wisely: Whether it's a tax refund, a bonus at work, or a monetary gift, consider putting a significant portion of windfalls into your emergency fund or other savings accounts. While treating yourself is okay, it's essential to strike a balance between enjoyment and financial prudence.

5. Explore Tax-Advantaged Accounts: Take advantage of retirement accounts and other tax-advantaged investment options to maximize your savings. Contributing to retirement accounts not only lowers your taxable income but also allows your money to grow tax-free or tax-deferred over time.

6. Consider High-Interest Savings Accounts: Look for savings accounts with higher interest rates. While the difference may seem small initially, over time, it can lead to substantial growth in your savings.

Managing Unexpected Financial Challenges
Even with a well-built emergency fund, unexpected financial challenges can still arise. How you handle these challenges can significantly impact your financial well-being. Here are some tips to manage unexpected situations:

1. Stay Calm and Assess the Situation: When facing a financial crisis, take a deep breath and assess the situation calmly. Understanding the full extent of the challenge will help you make informed decisions.

2. Prioritize Essential Expenses: Identify your essential expenses and prioritize them. These might include housing, utilities, food, and healthcare. Cut back on non-essential expenses temporarily to free up more funds for critical needs.

3. Explore Additional Income Streams: If possible, consider finding additional sources of income to supplement your savings during challenging times. This could involve taking up freelance work, selling items you no longer need, or exploring part-time opportunities.

4. Communicate with Creditors: If you find yourself struggling to meet debt obligations, communicate with your creditors. Many lenders are willing to work with you during difficult times and may offer alternative payment arrangements.

5. Avoid Draining Your Entire Emergency Fund: While it's essential to use your emergency fund for genuine emergencies, try to avoid depleting it entirely. Keeping a portion intact ensures you have a safety net for future uncertainties.

6. Learn from the Experience: Use the unexpected challenge as an opportunity to learn and grow. Analyze what led to the situation and take steps to prevent similar occurrences in the future.

Remember, building a strong saving and emergency fund is an ongoing process. Stay committed to your financial goals, and over time, you'll enjoy the security and peace of mind that comes with knowing you're well-prepared for whatever life throws your way. Happy saving!

Making Smart Investments and Growing Your Wealth

While budgeting and saving are crucial components of financial success, investing is the key to building long-term prosperity. We will explore different investment options, building a diversified portfolio, and the importance of seeking professional financial advice. So, let's embark on this journey to unlock the potential of your hard-earned money and make it work for you.

Understanding Different Investment Options

Before you jump into the investment realm, it's essential to understand the various options available. Investments can take various forms, each with its unique characteristics, risk profile, and potential returns. Let's explore some common investment avenues:

1. Stocks: Investing in individual company stocks means buying a piece of ownership in that company. Stocks can yield substantial returns over time, but they come with higher risk and volatility. It's crucial to research and choose companies with strong fundamentals and growth potential.

2. Bonds: Bonds are debt securities issued by governments or corporations. When you buy a bond, you lend money to the issuer for a specified period in exchange for interest payments. Bonds are generally considered safer than stocks, but the returns are often lower.

3. Mutual Funds: Mutual funds pool money from multiple investors to invest in a diversified portfolio of stocks, bonds, or other assets. They offer professional management and diversification, making them a popular choice for many investors.

4. Exchange-Traded Funds (ETFs): Similar to mutual funds, ETFs hold a collection of assets, but they trade on stock exchanges like individual stocks. ETFs provide liquidity and flexibility, making them an attractive option for both short-term and long-term investors.

5. Real Estate: Investing in real estate involves buying properties for rental income or capital appreciation. Real estate can provide a steady income stream and act as a hedge against inflation.

6. Retirement Accounts: Retirement accounts, such as 401(k)s and IRAs, offer tax advantages for long-term savings. They allow you to invest in various assets while enjoying tax benefits until you withdraw the funds during retirement.

Building a Diversified Investment Portfolio
Diversification is a fundamental principle of investing. It involves spreading your money across different asset classes to reduce risk and increase potential returns. A diversified portfolio typically includes a mix of stocks, bonds, real estate, and other investment vehicles. Here's how to build a well-rounded investment portfolio:

1. Assess Your Risk Tolerance: Before creating your portfolio, determine how much risk you are willing to take. Younger investors with a longer time horizon may tolerate higher risk for potentially higher returns, while those approaching retirement may prefer a more conservative approach.

2. Allocate Assets Strategically: Allocate your funds across different asset classes based on your risk tolerance, investment goals, and time horizon. The right asset allocation will depend on your financial situation and objectives.

3. Monitor and Rebalance: Regularly review your portfolio to ensure it aligns with your investment strategy.

Over time, some assets may outperform others, leading to an unbalanced portfolio. Rebalancing involves selling some investments and buying others to maintain your desired asset allocation.

Seeking Professional Financial Advice
Investing can be complex, and it's natural to seek guidance from professionals who specialize in financial planning and investment management. Here are some reasons why seeking professional advice is essential:

1. Expertise and Knowledge: Financial advisors have in-depth knowledge of the investment landscape and can guide you through various options based on your financial goals and risk tolerance.

2. Personalized Advice: An experienced advisor will take the time to understand your unique financial situation and tailor investment recommendations to suit your needs.

3. Long-Term Planning: Financial advisors can help you create a comprehensive financial plan that goes beyond investments, addressing other aspects like retirement planning, tax strategies, and estate planning.

4. Emotional Discipline: During market turbulence, emotions can cloud investment decisions. A financial advisor can provide objective advice and help you stay focused on your long-term goals.

You've now gained a better understanding of different investment options, building a diversified portfolio, and the benefits of seeking professional financial advice. Remember, investing is a journey that requires patience, discipline, and continuous learning. Always stay informed, monitor your investments, and adapt your strategy as needed. With time and the right approach, your investments can grow and pave the way to achieving your financial dreams. Happy investing!

Chapter 5: Developing Healthy Money Habits

Cultivating Mindful Spending and Financial Discipline

In our fast-paced and consumer-driven world, it's easy to fall into the trap of mindless spending and lose sight of our long-term financial goals. However, by cultivating mindful spending and financial discipline, we can build a solid foundation for a secure and prosperous future. In this section, we'll explore key practices that will help you differentiate between needs and wants, embrace delayed gratification, and stay accountable to your financial aspirations.

Differentiating Between Needs and Wants

One of the first steps in cultivating mindful spending is learning to differentiate between needs and wants. Needs are the essential things required for survival and well-being, such as food, shelter, clothing, and healthcare. Wants, on the other hand, are desires and luxuries that can enhance our lives but are not essential for survival.

To begin, take some time to evaluate your current spending habits. Ask yourself if your purchases are driven by genuine needs or if they are influenced by societal pressures or fleeting desires. By understanding the difference, you can start making conscious choices about where you allocate your hard-earned money.

Practicing mindful spending also involves creating a budget that aligns with your financial goals. Allocate a portion of your income to cover necessities and essential expenses, and then designate a separate portion for discretionary spending on wants. By doing this, you can avoid overspending on things that provide short-term satisfaction but little long-term value.

At times, it can be challenging to distinguish between what we truly need and what we desire in the moment. Needs are the essentials required for our survival, safety, and well-being, while wants are often driven by impulses and short-term desires. To develop mindful spending habits, start by evaluating each expense through a critical lens.

Take Stock of Your Priorities: Begin by creating a list of your essential needs, such as housing, utilities, food, and healthcare. Understanding your core priorities will help you allocate your resources more consciously.

Pause and Reflect Before Purchasing: When faced with a potential purchase, take a moment to pause and consider if it aligns with your needs and long-term financial objectives. Impulse buying can lead to unnecessary expenses that hinder your progress towards financial stability.

Practice the 24-Hour Rule: Before making a significant purchase, give yourself a 24-hour cooling-off period. This time allows you to reflect on whether the purchase is genuinely essential or if it's a momentary desire that may not hold its appeal in the long run.

Practicing Delayed Gratification for Long-Term Benefits
In a world of instant gratification, developing the habit of delayed gratification can be transformative for your financial well-being. Delayed gratification involves resisting immediate rewards in favor of more substantial, long-term benefits.

Set Specific Financial Goals: Outline clear and measurable financial goals, both short-term and long-term. Having a roadmap of your objectives will make it easier to prioritize delayed gratification over instant indulgence.

Create a Reward System: As you work towards your goals, devise a reward system to treat yourself when specific milestones are achieved. These rewards should be meaningful but not detrimental to your financial progress.

Focus on the Bigger Picture: Remind yourself of the greater purpose behind your financial aspirations. Whether it's building an emergency fund, purchasing a home, or securing a comfortable retirement, staying focused on the bigger picture will help you overcome the temptation of immediate spending.

Staying Accountable to Your Financial Goals
Accountability is a vital aspect of developing healthy money habits. It's essential to establish structures that keep you on track and help you course-correct when necessary.

Create a Budget: A well-crafted budget is a powerful tool for financial discipline. Track your income and expenses diligently, ensuring that your spending aligns with your financial plan.

Review Your Progress Regularly: Schedule regular check-ins with yourself to review your financial progress. Celebrate achievements, identify areas for improvement, and make adjustments as needed.

Seek Support and Share Goals: Share your financial goals with a trusted friend, family member, or financial advisor. Having someone to hold you accountable and provide encouragement can make a significant difference in staying disciplined.

Developing mindful spending habits and financial discipline is a journey that requires dedication and self-awareness. Remember, every small step you take today can have a profound impact on your financial well-being tomorrow. So, take charge of your financial habits and build a brighter and more abundant tomorrow.

Eliminating Debt and Managing Credit Wisely

In this section, we will delve into the critical aspect of developing healthy money habits by effectively managing debt and credit. Debt can be a significant burden on our financial well-being, and understanding how to eliminate it while managing credit wisely is essential for achieving long-term financial success and abundance.

Creating a Debt Repayment Strategy

Debt is a common challenge that many people face in their financial journeys. Whether it's student loans, credit card debt, or personal loans, being burdened by debt can hold us back from achieving our financial goals. The first step in eliminating debt is to create a debt repayment strategy.

To start, gather all the information about your outstanding debts, including the amount owed, interest rates, and minimum monthly payments. Next, analyze your monthly budget to determine how much extra money you can allocate towards debt repayment. Consider cutting back on discretionary spending and finding ways to increase your income, like taking up a part-time job or freelancing.

Once you have a clear understanding of your finances, choose a debt repayment approach that suits your situation. Two popular methods are the "Debt Snowball" and the "Debt Avalanche." The Debt Snowball method involves paying off the smallest debts first, while making minimum payments on other debts. As each small debt is paid off, the extra money is rolled into the next debt, creating momentum. The Debt Avalanche method, on the other hand, focuses on paying off debts with the highest interest rates first, saving more money on interest in the long run.

Regardless of the approach you choose, consistency is key. Stick to your repayment plan diligently and celebrate each debt milestone as you make progress. Eliminating debt not only lightens the financial load but also frees up money to invest in wealth-building opportunities.

The key to regaining control of your finances is to create a debt repayment strategy tailored to your unique circumstances. Here's how to get started:

Assess Your Debts: Begin by gathering all the information about your debts, including outstanding balances, interest rates, and minimum monthly payments. This knowledge will serve as the foundation for your repayment plan.

Prioritize High-Interest Debts: Tackle high-interest debts first. Allocate more funds to repay these debts while making minimum payments on others. Paying off high-interest debts quickly will save you money in the long run.

Negotiate with Creditors: Don't be afraid to negotiate with creditors or lenders to lower interest rates or set up a more manageable payment plan. Many creditors are willing to work with you if they see your commitment to clearing your debts.

Avoid New Debt: While repaying existing debt, avoid accumulating new debt. Cut down on unnecessary expenses and explore ways to increase your income to expedite the debt repayment process.

Reducing Credit Card Dependency and Interest Payments

Credit cards can be both a blessing and a curse. They offer convenience and rewards, but they also come with high-interest rates that can trap us in a cycle of debt. To manage credit cards wisely, it's essential to reduce credit card dependency and interest payments.

Start by reviewing your credit card statements to understand your spending habits and identify areas where you can cut back. Create a budget and allocate specific amounts for different expenses, ensuring you spend within your means. Avoid using credit cards for everyday purchases if possible, and opt for cash or debit cards instead.

If you already carry credit card debt, focus on paying more than the minimum monthly payment. Even a small increase in payments can significantly reduce the time it takes to pay off the balance and save you money on interest charges. Consider transferring high-interest credit card balances to a card with a lower interest rate or explore debt consolidation options to streamline multiple debts into a single manageable payment.

Resist the temptation to accumulate more debt by making impulsive purchases. Before using your credit card, ask yourself if the purchase is necessary and if you have the means to pay it off in full when the statement arrives.

Building a Strong Credit Score
Your credit score is a critical factor that lenders use to assess your creditworthiness. A high credit score can open doors to better interest rates on loans, credit cards, and even impact your ability to rent an apartment or get a job. Building a strong credit score requires responsible credit management.

Start by obtaining a free copy of your credit report from each of the major credit bureaus: Equifax, Experian, and TransUnion. Review the reports for inaccuracies, such as incorrect account information or late payments. Dispute any errors you find to ensure your credit report reflects accurate information.

To build a strong credit score, focus on paying your bills on time, every time. Payment history is one of the most significant factors influencing your credit score. Set up automatic payments or reminders to ensure you never miss a due date.

Keep your credit card balances low relative to your credit limits, as this demonstrates responsible credit utilization. Aim to use no more than 30% of your available credit at any given time.

Avoid opening multiple new credit accounts within a short period, as this can lower your average account age and impact your score negatively. Choose credit accounts that align with your financial needs and goals.

Developing healthy money habits involves managing debt responsibly and handling credit wisely. By creating a debt repayment strategy, reducing credit card dependency, and building a strong credit score, you take significant steps towards achieving financial freedom and abundance. Remember, it's not just about making money but also managing it wisely to create a secure and prosperous future.

Navigating Through Financial Challenges and Setbacks

Life is full of unexpected twists and turns, and financial crises can hit us when we least expect them. But fear not! With the right strategies and a resilient mindset, you can overcome these challenges and use them as stepping stones towards a brighter financial future.

Coping with Unexpected Financial Crises

Life has a way of throwing us curveballs, and financial crises can emerge suddenly, catching us off guard. These crises could be in the form of medical emergencies, job loss, natural disasters, or any unforeseen circumstance that puts a strain on our finances.

Financial crises can take many forms, such as sudden job loss, medical emergencies, or unforeseen expenses. Coping with these challenges requires a combination of emotional strength and practical planning. Here are some steps to help you navigate through unexpected financial crises:

1. Stay Calm and Assess the Situation: When faced with a financial crisis, it's natural to feel overwhelmed or anxious. Take a deep breath and assess the situation objectively. Understand the severity of the crisis, the available resources, and the potential solutions.

2. Build a Support Network: Reach out to friends, family, or support groups for emotional and practical support. Sometimes, sharing the burden can lighten the load and provide fresh perspectives on potential solutions.

3. Prioritize Expenses: Identify essential expenses, such as housing, utilities, and food, and prioritize them over non-essential ones. Trim unnecessary costs and focus on conserving resources until the situation stabilizes.

4. Negotiate with Creditors: If you're struggling to meet debt obligations, communicate with your creditors. Many lenders offer hardship programs that can temporarily reduce payments or adjust interest rates during difficult times.

5. Explore Emergency Funds and Insurance: Having an emergency fund in place is crucial for handling unexpected crises. If you have insurance policies, such as health or disability insurance, familiarize yourself with the coverage and claims process.

Strategies for Bouncing Back from Financial Setbacks
Bouncing back from a financial setback requires resilience and a positive outlook. While it may not be easy, it's possible to emerge stronger than before. Here are some strategies to help you on your journey to recovery:

1. Set Realistic Goals: After experiencing a setback, reassess your financial goals and set realistic milestones. Break down larger objectives into smaller, achievable steps to regain your financial footing.

2. Create a Contingency Plan: Learn from the crisis and create a contingency plan for future challenges. Having a financial safety net and a clear action plan can reduce stress and build confidence in your ability to handle setbacks.

3. Build a Stronger Budget: Reevaluate your budget and identify areas where you can cut costs or allocate resources more efficiently. A well-balanced budget can help you manage your finances more effectively.

4. Focus on Building Savings: Prioritize rebuilding your emergency fund to protect against future uncertainties. Consistent saving, even if it's a small amount, can make a significant difference over time.

5. Explore New Opportunities: A setback can be an opportunity to explore new avenues for financial growth. Consider pursuing additional streams of income or leveraging your skills in different ways.

Learning from Financial Mistakes and Failures
Mistakes and failures are part of life, including financial ones. Instead of dwelling on the past, use these experiences as valuable lessons to improve your financial decision-making. Here's how you can learn from financial mistakes:

1. Take Responsibility: Acknowledge your mistakes and take responsibility for them. Avoid placing blame on external factors and focus on what you can control moving forward.

2. Analyze the Root Cause: Understand the reasons behind your financial mistakes. It could be impulsive spending, inadequate planning, or lack of financial knowledge. Identifying the root cause helps prevent repeating the same errors.

3. Seek Knowledge and Expert Advice: Educate yourself about personal finance and seek advice from financial experts. Knowledge is empowering, and learning from professionals can help you make informed decisions.

4. Set Up Systems to Avoid Repetition: Implement systems that prevent the recurrence of previous mistakes. For example, set up automatic savings to avoid overspending or create a budgeting app to track your expenses.

5. Practice Self-Compassion: Be kind to yourself during this process. Everyone makes mistakes, and the important thing is to learn from them and use the knowledge to make better choices in the future.

Remember, financial setbacks are temporary, and with determination and the right mindset, you can overcome them. Embrace the learning opportunities they offer, and use them to fuel your journey toward financial abundance.

Chapter 6: Giving Back and Sharing Your Wealth

The Joy of Giving: The Link Between Generosity and Wealth

In this chapter, we will explore the profound connection between generosity and wealth. Many successful individuals and entrepreneurs have discovered that giving back is not only a noble pursuit but also a powerful way to attract and maintain financial abundance in their lives.

Engaging in Philanthropy and Charitable Activities

One of the most fulfilling ways to share your wealth is through philanthropy and charitable activities. Engaging in acts of giving can transform your relationship with money and open doors to new opportunities. Philanthropy allows you to make a positive impact on the lives of others, contributing to causes that resonate with your values and passions.

When you participate in charitable activities, you become part of something greater than yourself. Whether you support education, healthcare, environmental conservation, or any other cause, your contributions can bring about significant change. The act of giving not only benefits the recipients but also provides a sense of purpose and fulfillment for the giver.

Generosity need not be limited to financial contributions alone; your time, skills, and expertise can also make a profound difference. Volunteering for local organizations or mentoring aspiring entrepreneurs can create a ripple effect of positive change that extends far beyond the immediate act of giving.

Supporting Causes Aligned with Your Values
In this interconnected world, there are countless causes and organizations that could use support. However, to experience the true joy of giving, it is essential to align your contributions with your values and passions. By supporting causes that resonate with you on a deeper level, you can create a meaningful connection to your philanthropic efforts.

Take the time to reflect on what matters most to you. Is it education, poverty alleviation, animal welfare, or promoting arts and culture? Identify the areas where you genuinely want to make a difference. Once you've found your cause, research organizations and initiatives that align with your values and are making a measurable impact.

Consider establishing a giving strategy that reflects your long-term commitment to the causes you care about. By focusing your efforts, you can maximize your impact and forge strong partnerships with organizations that share your vision.

The Ripple Effect of Giving and Its Impact on Abundance
The act of giving has a fascinating ripple effect on your life and the lives of others. When you give with a genuine heart, it creates a positive energy that radiates outward,

attracting more abundance into your life. This is often referred to as the Law of Reciprocity—by sharing your wealth and resources, you open yourself up to receiving more in return.

Giving also enhances your sense of gratitude and contentment. As you witness the positive change brought about by your contributions, you gain a deeper appreciation for the blessings in your life. This heightened sense of gratitude helps you attract even more abundance and opportunities.

Moreover, the act of giving inspires others to do the same. When people see the impact you are making, they are motivated to follow your example. Your generosity can create a domino effect, encouraging a network of giving that extends far beyond your own contributions.

Giving back and sharing your wealth is not only a noble endeavor but also a powerful way to attract and sustain financial abundance. Engaging in philanthropy and supporting causes aligned with your values can bring immense joy and fulfillment to your life. Remember that the act of giving is not solely about the amount you give, but the intention and impact behind your contributions. By fostering a culture of generosity and abundance, you create a positive ripple effect that touches the lives of many, including your own. So, let your heart guide your giving, and may your wealth be a force for positive change in the world.

Nurturing the Routine of Giving

Giving is not just an act of kindness; it's a powerful tool
that can amplify the flow of abundance in our lives and
enrich our overall sense of purpose and happiness. So, let's
dive into the art of nurturing a giving routine that will bring
about positive change in both our lives and the lives of
others.

The Transformative Power of Giving

Giving is a two-way street. When we give from the heart,
not only do we make a positive impact on someone else's
life, but we also experience a profound sense of fulfillment
and joy within ourselves. It's like magic - the more we give,
the more we receive. But remember, it's not just about the
money; giving can take many forms, including time, skills,
knowledge, and support.

The Energetics of Generosity and Abundance

Have you ever noticed that when you give freely, it feels
like the universe conspires to give back to you in
unexpected ways? That's because the act of giving creates a
positive energetic flow. When you give, you signal to the
universe that you have more than enough to share, and in
return, the universe responds by providing you with even
more abundance.

Giving is not just limited to financial contributions; it can
be as simple as offering a listening ear to a friend in need,
volunteering for a cause you're passionate about, or sharing

your skills to help someone overcome a challenge. When you approach giving with an open heart and a mindset of abundance, you create a powerful energy that attracts wealth and positivity into your life.

Finding Causes that Align with Your Passion and Purpose
To nurture a giving routine, it's essential to find causes that resonate with your values, passions, and purpose. When you support causes that align with your beliefs, it adds a deeper sense of meaning to your giving journey. Take some time to reflect on the issues that ignite your soul, whether it's environmental conservation, education, healthcare, or any other area that holds a special place in your heart.

Once you've identified your passions, seek out reputable organizations or initiatives that are making a real impact in those areas. Look for opportunities to volunteer your time or contribute your skills. Remember, giving doesn't always require monetary donations; your time and expertise can be equally valuable and rewarding.

Creating Social Enterprises with a Purpose-Driven Mission
If you have an entrepreneurial spirit, consider incorporating giving into your business model. Social enterprises are organizations that prioritize social and environmental goals alongside financial success. By blending profit with purpose, you can create a sustainable business that makes a positive difference in the world.

Whether it's committing a portion of your profits to charitable causes or directly integrating social impact into your product or service, a purpose-driven business can attract like-minded customers who want to support businesses with a conscience. Plus, running a socially responsible enterprise can fuel your motivation and passion for your work, leading to greater success and fulfillment.

Building a Routine of Giving

Now that we understand the transformative power of giving and the various ways to contribute, let's explore how to build a sustainable routine of giving that fits into our daily lives:

Start Small and Grow:

Like any habit, cultivating a giving routine takes time. Start by committing to small acts of kindness each week. It could be as simple as buying a coffee for the person behind you in line or donating a small amount to a charity you believe in. As you witness the positive impact of your actions, you'll naturally be inspired to do more.

Set Giving Goals:

Just as you set financial goals, create giving goals too. Decide how much time or money you want to contribute each month or year. Having specific giving targets will keep you focused and motivated to stay on track.

Integrate Giving into Your Budget:

Make giving a line item in your budget, just like any other expense. By setting aside a portion of your income for giving, you ensure that it becomes a consistent part of your financial plan.

Embrace Collaboration:

You don't have to give alone. Join forces with friends, family, or colleagues to support causes together. Collaborative giving not only increases your collective impact but also strengthens the bonds between you and your giving partners.

As we wrap up this section on nurturing the routine of giving, I encourage you to open your heart to the immense joy and fulfillment that comes from making a positive impact in the lives of others. Embrace giving as an essential part of your journey towards attracting abundance and building a harmonious relationship with money.

Giving is not just a one-time act; it's a lifestyle that brings purpose and meaning to our lives. Whether it's a small gesture or a significant contribution, your giving routine will not only enrich the lives of others but also create a ripple effect of abundance that will come back to bless you in countless ways. So, let's continue to nurture this beautiful practice of giving and watch as it brings greater wealth and fulfillment into our lives. Happy giving!

How Giving Can Contribute to Your Financial Freedom

When we think about achieving financial freedom, the first thing that often comes to mind is acquiring wealth and accumulating assets. However, there's a lesser-known secret to attaining true financial freedom - giving back and sharing your wealth with others. It might sound counterintuitive at first, but embracing a mindset of generosity and philanthropy can have a profound impact on your journey towards financial freedom. In this sub-chapter, we'll explore how giving can contribute to your financial well-being and abundance.

The Principle of Giving and Receiving

The age-old principle of giving and receiving forms the foundation of how giving back can lead to financial freedom. The idea is simple yet powerful - the more you give, the more you receive. When you give generously and without expectation, you create a positive flow of energy and abundance. This positive energy attracts more opportunities and blessings into your life, including financial ones.

1.The Law of Reciprocity

You might have heard the saying, "What goes around, comes around." Well, that's the essence of the Law of Reciprocity. This universal law states that when you give generously, the universe responds by giving back to you in

unexpected and abundant ways. It's like a boomerang
effect; the more you give, the more you receive. So,
embracing generosity is not only a selfless act, but it's also
an investment in your own future.

2.Creating an Abundance Mindset

When you're generous and open-handed with your wealth,
you're sending a powerful message to your subconscious
mind – that you have more than enough to share and that
you trust in the abundance of the universe. This mindset
shift is crucial in attracting more wealth into your life. By
affirming that you're abundant and have the capacity to
give, you're rewiring your brain to focus on opportunities
and possibilities, rather than scarcity and lack.

3.Giving as a Seed for Prosperity

Think of giving as planting seeds of prosperity. When you
sow seeds in fertile ground, you expect a bountiful harvest,
right? Well, the same principle applies to giving. When you
give with a genuine heart, you're sowing seeds of positivity,
gratitude, and goodwill. These seeds grow into a harvest of
blessings, and you'll be amazed at how the universe
conspires to multiply the goodness you've shared.

4.Building Stronger Connections and Networks

Generosity isn't just about giving money; it's also about giving your time, skills, and expertise. When you offer your help and support to others, you're building genuine connections and networks. These connections can lead to unexpected opportunities, collaborations, and friendships that can enrich your life in ways you never imagined. Remember, success is not just about what you know; it's also about who you know.

Giving Back to Yourself
Yes, you read that right! Giving back to yourself is an essential aspect of the giving equation. It's important to strike a balance between being generous to others and taking care of your own needs. When you prioritize self-care and well-being, you're better equipped to continue giving without burning out. Remember the old saying, "You can't pour from an empty cup." So, ensure your cup is full first, so you can continue making a positive impact.

Giving Beyond Money
While financial donations are valuable, giving goes beyond money. Your time, knowledge, and skills are equally precious resources that can make a significant impact. Mentoring someone, sharing your expertise, or simply being there to listen and support can be life-changing for someone else. Embrace the power of your unique gifts and talents to make a difference in the lives of others.

Giving back not only makes a difference in the lives of others, but it also enriches our own lives in ways we could never have imagined. As you journey towards financial freedom, remember that generosity is a key that unlocks the doors to abundance. So, let's make the world a better place, one act of kindness at a time!

Chapter 7 - Attracting Money through Positive Energy

Harnessing Positive Energy for Financial Attraction

Hey there, welcome to Chapter 7! In this exciting section, we'll delve into the fascinating world of attracting money through positive energy. It's time to discover how your mindset and environment can play a significant role in drawing financial abundance into your life. So, let's dive right in!

Understanding the Connection Between Energy and Money

You might have heard the saying, "Like attracts like." Well, that applies to money too! The energy you emit through your thoughts, emotions, and actions can profoundly influence your financial outcomes. It's all about the law of attraction - the idea that positive or negative thoughts bring positive or negative experiences into your life.

When you cultivate a positive and abundant mindset, you become a magnet for prosperity. Believe that money is a positive force in your life, and that it can be used to create opportunities and make a difference in the world. Embrace a mindset that fosters gratitude, abundance, and generosity, and you'll be amazed at how the universe responds in kind.

Clearing Financial Clutter and Creating Space for Abundance

Now that you understand the power of positive energy, let's address a critical aspect of attracting money - clearing financial clutter. Clutter isn't just about physical possessions; it extends to your financial life too. Unresolved debts, messy financial records, and disorganized spending habits can create negative energy that hinders financial flow.

Take a deep breath and declutter your financial space. Start by organizing your bills, creating a budget, and setting clear financial goals. Tackle outstanding debts strategically and develop a plan to pay them off systematically. As you clear this financial clutter, you'll make room for abundance to flow effortlessly into your life.

Practicing Feng Shui for Prosperity

Feng Shui, the ancient Chinese art of arranging your environment to harmonize with the flow of energy, can be a powerful tool for attracting prosperity. By making simple adjustments to your living and workspace, you can enhance the flow of positive energy and invite financial abundance into your life.

1. The Power of the Wealth Corner: In Feng Shui, the southeast corner of your home or office represents wealth and abundance. Keep this area clean, clutter-free, and vibrant. Add symbols of prosperity, such as a money plant or a bowl of coins, to amplify its energy.

2. Fixing Leaks and Drips: In Feng Shui, water represents wealth. Fix any leaky faucets or plumbing issues promptly, as they symbolize money "leaking" away. By addressing these problems, you'll signal the universe that you're taking charge of your finances.

3. Welcoming the Chi: The entrance to your home or office is where energy, or chi, enters. Ensure it's well-lit, clutter-free, and inviting. A vibrant doormat and a healthy, thriving plant can attract positive energy and prosperity into your space.

4. Mirrors and Abundance: Mirrors are considered powerful amplifiers in Feng Shui. Place mirrors strategically to reflect abundance and opportunities. Avoid placing mirrors facing the main door, as it might push positive energy away.

5. Live Plants and Prosperity: Living plants symbolize growth and vitality. Incorporate lush, healthy plants into your living and workspace to promote financial growth and prosperity.

6. Declutter with Purpose: A cluttered space can block the flow of energy. Clear out items that no longer serve a purpose, and let go of old, negative energy. As you declutter, make room for new opportunities and abundance.

Remember, Feng Shui is about creating harmony and balance in your environment. Apply these principles with intention and positivity, and watch as the energy of prosperity begins to flow effortlessly into your life.

Congratulations! You've taken the first steps towards harnessing positive energy for financial attraction. By understanding the connection between energy and money, clearing financial clutter, and incorporating Feng Shui practices, you're setting yourself up for a prosperous and abundant journey. Embrace this positive energy, stay open to opportunities, and remember that you have the power to attract financial abundance into your life!

Aligning Your Actions with Financial Goals

In this section, we will explore how to align your actions with your financial goals to attract abundance and prosperity. Remember, the key to unlocking the flow of money lies not only in changing your thoughts but also in taking inspired action to manifest your dreams. So, let's dive in and discover how you can align your actions with financial success!

Taking Inspired Action Towards Financial Success

Creating a strong money mindset is a fantastic start, but it's the actions you take that will determine the trajectory of your financial journey. When you align your actions with your financial goals, you signal to the universe that you are ready to receive the abundance you desire. Here are some powerful ways to take inspired action towards financial success:

a. Set Clear and Specific Goals: The journey to financial abundance begins with defining your goals. Be clear about what you want to achieve financially, whether it's paying off debt, building a savings buffer, or investing in your dream business. Write down your goals and break them into smaller, achievable steps.

b. Create a Vision Board: Visualization is a potent tool in manifesting your desires. Design a vision board that represents your financial goals. Include images that inspire you, affirmations that resonate with your intentions, and symbols of wealth and prosperity. Place your vision board in a prominent spot where you can see it daily.

c. Take Daily Inspired Action: Consistent, small steps can lead to significant progress over time. Take inspired action every day towards your financial goals. Whether it's saving a percentage of your income, researching investment opportunities, or learning new skills to enhance your earning potential, each action contributes to your financial success.

d. Embrace a Growth Mindset: Be open to learning and growing in your financial journey. Challenges and setbacks are inevitable, but with a growth mindset, you view them as opportunities to learn and improve. Embrace a mindset of continuous improvement, and you'll be better equipped to overcome obstacles and keep moving forward.

Making Financial Decisions from an Empowered State

Empowerment is a vital aspect of attracting money through positive energy. When you make financial decisions from a place of strength and confidence, you send a powerful message to the universe that you are in control of your financial destiny. Here's how you can make financial decisions from an empowered state:

a. Cultivate Self-Trust: Trust yourself and your ability to make sound financial decisions. Avoid seeking constant validation from others, as it can cloud your judgment. Instead, rely on your knowledge, experience, and intuition to guide you in making the right choices for your financial future.

b. Stay Informed: Knowledge is power, especially in financial matters. Stay informed about personal finance, investing, and money management. Attend workshops, read books, and seek advice from reputable financial experts. The more informed you are, the better equipped you'll be to make informed decisions.

c. Tune Into Your Values: Consider your values and life priorities when making financial choices. Ask yourself if a particular expense aligns with your values and brings you closer to your goals. Making decisions in line with your values not only empowers you but also brings a sense of purpose and fulfillment to your financial journey.

d. Avoid Hasty Decisions: Impulsive decisions can lead to regret and financial strain. Take your time to evaluate options, seek advice if needed, and sleep on major decisions. Give yourself the space to make well-thought-out choices that align with your long-term vision.

Combining Intuition and Rationality in Money Matters
Intuition and rationality may seem like opposing forces, but when combined, they create a powerful decision-making tool. Trusting your gut instincts while also considering logical factors can lead to well-balanced and successful outcomes. Here's how you can find harmony between intuition and rationality in money matters:

a. Practice Mindfulness and Inner Listening: Develop mindfulness practices to quiet the noise around you and connect with your inner self. When making financial decisions, take a moment to listen to your intuition. Often, your inner voice provides valuable insights that logic alone may overlook.

b. Analyze the Numbers: While intuition plays a crucial role, financial decisions also require a rational assessment of the numbers. Analyze the financial data, compare options, and evaluate potential risks and returns. Combining intuition with logical analysis allows you to make informed decisions that feel right and make sense financially.

c. Trust Your Past Experiences: Your past experiences can serve as valuable guides. Reflect on past financial decisions and their outcomes. Consider what worked well and what didn't. Trust the lessons you've learned from previous experiences to inform your present choices.

d. Surround Yourself with Supportive Voices: Seek advice and support from like-minded individuals who understand and respect the power of combining intuition and rationality. Engaging in discussions with supportive friends or joining financial groups can provide valuable insights and broaden your perspectives.

Aligning your actions with your financial goals involves taking inspired action, making decisions from an empowered state, and finding harmony between intuition and rationality. As you embrace these practices, you'll witness the powerful synergy between your positive energy and the flow of money. Trust the process, stay committed to your vision, and know that financial abundance is within your reach. Keep moving forward with confidence, and watch as the universe aligns to support your journey towards prosperity.

Cultivating a Mindset of Worthiness and Deservingness

Many individuals struggle with money-related issues due to deep-seated beliefs about their self-worth and whether they truly deserve financial prosperity. However, by recognizing your inherent value, releasing guilt and shame around money, and affirming your right to abundance, you can transform your relationship with money and create a powerful energy of attraction.

Recognizing Your Inherent Value and Deservingness of Wealth

At the core of attracting money through positive energy lies the belief that you are inherently deserving of financial abundance. Understand that your self-worth is not tied to your net worth; rather, it is an inherent aspect of your being. You are worthy of wealth and prosperity simply because you exist. Embrace the truth that you are a unique and valuable individual, possessing talents, skills, and potential that contribute positively to the world.

To recognize your inherent value, practice self-compassion and kindness towards yourself. Treat yourself with the same love and care that you would extend to a dear friend. Acknowledge your strengths and accomplishments, no matter how small they may seem. Celebrate your efforts and progress, understanding that every step forward, no matter how small, is a testament to your growth.

Releasing Guilt and Shame Around Money

Guilt and shame surrounding money can be significant barriers to financial well-being. These emotions often arise from past experiences or societal conditioning, leading to negative associations with wealth and success. To attract money through positive energy, it's essential to release these emotions and replace them with a healthier perspective.

Begin by exploring the root causes of any guilt or shame you feel about money. Recognize that financial struggles or past mistakes do not define your future potential. Forgive yourself for any perceived financial shortcomings, understanding that mistakes are a natural part of the learning process.

It's important to remember that money is a tool that can be used for both personal growth and making a positive impact on the world. By cultivating a healthy relationship with money, you empower yourself to contribute positively to your life and the lives of others.

Affirming Your Right to Abundance

Affirmations are powerful tools that can help you shift your mindset and attract positive energy. Affirmations are positive statements that you can repeat daily to reinforce your beliefs and intentions. When it comes to money, affirmations can be especially transformative.

Create personal affirmations that affirm your right to abundance. For example:

"I am worthy of financial prosperity and success."

"Money flows easily and effortlessly into my life."

"I release all limiting beliefs about money and embrace my true abundance."

Repeat these affirmations daily, either silently or aloud, and visualize yourself experiencing the abundance you desire. By consistently reinforcing these positive beliefs, you'll gradually align your subconscious mind with your conscious desire for financial abundance.

Additionally, take inspired action towards your financial goals. The combination of positive affirmations and proactive steps towards financial success creates a powerful synergy that propels you closer to your aspirations.

Attracting money through positive energy begins with cultivating a mindset of worthiness and deservingness. Recognize your inherent value, release guilt and shame around money, and affirm your right to abundance. Remember that positive energy attracts positive outcomes, and by aligning your thoughts, emotions, and actions with prosperity, you can create a fulfilling and abundant financial reality. Trust in your ability to attract money, and watch as the universe responds in kind.

Chapter 8: Building and Sustaining Wealth Habits

Developing Long-Term Wealth-Building Habits

In this section, we will delve into the key aspects of developing long-term wealth-building habits that will pave the way to a brighter and more abundant financial future. Building a strong foundation through consistency, automation, and setting healthy boundaries is the secret sauce to financial success.

The Power of Consistency in Financial Success

Consistency is the driving force behind achieving any goal, and it holds especially true when it comes to financial success. Just like any other habit, managing your finances requires discipline and dedication. Cultivating consistent financial habits allows you to stay focused on your objectives and empowers you to make well-informed decisions.

1. Establishing a Routine: One of the first steps to being consistent with your finances is to create a routine. Set aside a specific time each week or month to review your budget, track expenses, and assess your progress towards your financial goals. Consistency breeds accountability and ensures you stay on top of your financial game.

2. Mindful Spending: Consistency involves aligning your spending with your financial goals. Make it a habit to evaluate your purchases and ask yourself whether they contribute to your long-term objectives. Being mindful of your spending patterns allows you to identify areas where you can cut back and redirect those funds towards saving and investing.

3. Patience and Perseverance: Rome wasn't built in a day, and neither is financial success. It requires patience and perseverance to stay the course, especially during challenging times. Don't be discouraged by setbacks; instead, view them as opportunities to learn and grow. Consistent effort, even in small increments, will yield substantial results over time.

Automating Savings and Investments

Automating your savings and investments is a game-changer in wealth-building. With the rise of digital banking and investment platforms, it has become easier than ever to set up automatic transfers and contributions. By automating these processes, you remove the temptation to spend the money elsewhere and ensure that you consistently put money towards your financial goals.

1. Pay Yourself First: Treat your savings and investments as non-negotiable expenses. When your paycheck comes in, allocate a portion directly into your savings and investment accounts before addressing other expenses. This concept of "paying yourself first" ensures that you prioritize your financial future over impulsive spending.

2. Emergency Fund Automation: Building an emergency fund is a critical aspect of financial security. Automate a portion of your income to be deposited into your emergency fund regularly. Having a safety net for unexpected expenses provides peace of mind and protects your long-term financial plans from being derailed.

3. Retirement Savings: Time flies, and retirement will sneak up sooner than you think. Take advantage of employer-sponsored retirement plans or individual retirement accounts (IRAs) and automate contributions. The power of compounding over the long term will significantly boost your retirement savings.

Setting Financial Boundaries and Prioritizing Financial Health
Building and sustaining wealth also involves setting boundaries to protect your financial health. Creating a clear understanding of your financial priorities and goals will help you make more intentional decisions and ensure that you are always working towards your vision of financial abundance.

1. Defining Financial Boundaries: It's essential to establish financial boundaries that align with your values and long-term objectives. This might mean saying "no" to unnecessary expenses that don't serve your financial goals or learning to set limits on supporting others financially. Setting boundaries empowers you to take control of your financial life.

2. Diversifying Your Assets: Spreading your investments across various asset classes reduces risk and enhances your overall financial security. Diversification is a key aspect of financial planning, as it allows you to benefit from different market conditions while mitigating potential losses.

3. Building Resilience: Financial setbacks are a part of life, and building resilience is crucial to navigate through them. A strong financial foundation with savings and investments acts as a buffer during challenging times, providing you with the confidence to face unexpected situations.

Developing long-term wealth-building habits is the cornerstone of financial success. Consistency, automation, and setting healthy financial boundaries will help you achieve your financial goals and create a prosperous future. Remember, small steps taken consistently can lead to significant financial transformations. Stay committed, be patient, and enjoy the journey towards financial freedom.

Staying Grounded Amid Financial Success

You've been working hard on your money mindset, setting clear financial goals, and creating multiple streams of income. As you see the fruits of your efforts and experience financial success, it's essential to stay grounded and maintain a healthy relationship with money. In this sub-chapter, we'll explore three vital aspects of staying grounded amid financial success: avoiding lifestyle inflation and keeping financial balance, cultivating humility and gratitude in wealth accumulation, and nurturing meaningful relationships beyond money.

Avoiding Lifestyle Inflation and Keeping Financial Balance

Lifestyle inflation, also known as lifestyle creep, is a common pitfall that many people face when they experience an increase in income. It refers to the tendency to increase spending as earnings rise, often leading to unnecessary expenses and financial imbalances. Avoiding lifestyle inflation is crucial to maintaining financial stability and building lasting wealth.

Key Point 1: Mindful Spending and Smart Choices

As your income grows, it's tempting to upgrade various aspects of your life, from buying a bigger house to purchasing luxury items. While treating yourself occasionally is fine, it's essential to make mindful spending choices. Consider whether a purchase aligns with your long-term financial goals and values. Think about whether it brings genuine happiness and adds value to your life. By prioritizing mindful spending, you can avoid wasteful expenses and direct your money towards experiences and items that truly matter to you.

Key Point 2: Save and Invest the Difference

Instead of spending the entirety of your increased income, consider saving and investing the difference. Continue living below your means, even as your earnings rise. This approach allows you to build a robust financial cushion, invest in your future, and achieve financial freedom more

quickly. Saving and investing the difference also provides
you with a sense of security, knowing that you have funds
set aside for unexpected situations or opportunities.

Key Point 3: Set Financial Boundaries

While it's great to be generous and help others, it's crucial
to set financial boundaries with family and friends. As your
financial success becomes apparent, you might encounter
requests for loans or financial assistance. While it's
admirable to support your loved ones, it's essential to strike
a balance between helping them and protecting your
financial stability. Consider offering support in non-
monetary ways, such as providing guidance or helping
them find resources to improve their financial situation.

**Cultivating Humility and Gratitude in Wealth
Accumulation**

As you amass wealth and achieve your financial goals, it's
essential to cultivate humility and gratitude. Recognize that
financial success is not solely a result of individual effort
but may also be influenced by external factors such as
opportunities, mentors, and luck. Staying humble and
grateful allows you to appreciate what you have while
remaining open to continuous growth.

Key Point 1: Reflect on Your Financial Journey

Take time to reflect on your financial journey and acknowledge the progress you've made. Celebrate the milestones and achievements, no matter how small they may seem. Embrace the lessons learned from any financial challenges or setbacks, as they have contributed to your growth and resilience.

Key Point 2: Give Back and Pay It Forward

Practicing gratitude can be amplified by giving back to your community and helping those in need. Engage in philanthropic activities or volunteer for causes you care about. Supporting others not only makes a positive impact on their lives but also enriches your sense of purpose and fulfillment.

Key Point 3: Stay Curious and Keep Learning

Cultivate a mindset of continuous learning and curiosity. The journey to financial success is not a one-time accomplishment; it's an ongoing process of growth and adaptation. Stay open to new ideas, explore different investment opportunities, and seek advice from financial experts to enhance your financial knowledge and decision-making.

Nurturing Meaningful Relationships Beyond Money
While financial success can bring numerous benefits, it's crucial to nurture relationships that go beyond monetary transactions. True wealth extends to meaningful connections and experiences with family, friends, and your community.

Key Point 1: Quality Time and Shared Experiences

Invest time and effort into building and maintaining meaningful relationships. Engage in activities that foster genuine connections and shared experiences. Remember that quality time spent with loved ones often outweighs lavish gifts or financial gestures.

Key Point 2: Support and Empowerment

Support your loved ones in their endeavors and encourage their personal growth. True wealth is not just about accumulating money for oneself but also empowering others to achieve their goals and dreams.

Key Point 3: Celebrate Success Together

Share your successes and celebrate the accomplishments of those around you. By celebrating together, you strengthen bonds and create a supportive and joyful environment.

Staying grounded amid financial success is not about restricting yourself or feeling guilty about prosperity. It's about finding a balance that allows you to enjoy the fruits of your labor while maintaining financial stability, cultivating gratitude, and nurturing meaningful relationships. With a healthy and balanced approach to wealth accumulation, you can continue to attract abundance into your life while living a fulfilled and purposeful existence.

Creating a Legacy of Financial Empowerment

As we journey towards financial abundance, it becomes essential not only to secure our own prosperity but also to create a lasting impact for future generations. Building a legacy of financial empowerment involves imparting valuable knowledge, contributing to the greater good, and fostering a culture of financial literacy and independence. In this sub-chapter, we'll explore three key ways to create a legacy that goes beyond just accumulating wealth – educating the next generation about money management, leaving a lasting impact through charitable endeavors, and fostering a culture of financial empowerment.

Educating the Next Generation about Money Management

Teaching the younger generation about money management is one of the most significant gifts we can give them. By providing them with essential financial knowledge early on, we empower them to make informed decisions and navigate the complex world of finances confidently.

1. Start Early: The journey to financial literacy begins at home. Introduce children to the concept of money, savings, and budgeting from a young age. Engage them in discussions about money matters in age-appropriate ways, and help them set simple savings goals for their pocket money.

2. Instill Healthy Money Habits: Encourage children to save a portion of their earnings or gifts. Teach them about delayed gratification and the importance of distinguishing between needs and wants. As they grow older, involve them in creating a budget and managing their expenses.

3. Introduce Investing: As kids become teenagers, introduce them to the basics of investing. Explain the power of compound interest and the different investment options available. Instill confidence in them to take calculated risks and use money as a tool for growth.

Leaving a Lasting Impact through Charitable Endeavors
Giving back to the community and supporting causes that align with our values can leave a powerful legacy of compassion and positive change. Engaging in charitable endeavors not only creates a lasting impact on the lives of others but also brings a sense of fulfillment and purpose to our own lives.

1. Identify Causes Close to Your Heart: Reflect on the issues that resonate with you and align with your values. Whether it's supporting education, healthcare, environmental conservation, or any other cause, choose organizations that genuinely make a difference.

2. Philanthropy with Purpose: Beyond financial contributions, consider offering your time, skills, or expertise to these causes. Engage in volunteer work or mentorship programs to directly impact the lives of those in need.

3. Create a Giving Plan: Establish a structured giving plan that aligns with your financial goals and capacity. Regularly contribute to the causes you support, and involve your family in the decision-making process to instill a sense of collective responsibility.

Fostering a Culture of Financial Empowerment
Beyond personal success, creating a legacy of financial empowerment involves inspiring and supporting others on their financial journeys. By fostering a culture of financial empowerment in our communities, workplaces, and families, we can uplift others and strengthen the foundation of our society.

1. Lead by Example: Be transparent about your financial journey and share your successes and challenges. This openness can inspire others to take charge of their finances and work towards their goals.

2. Organize Workshops and Seminars: Collaborate with local organizations or community centers to conduct workshops and seminars on financial literacy. Cover topics such as budgeting, investing, debt management, and retirement planning.

3. Support Financial Education Initiatives: Advocate for improved financial education in schools and colleges. Support organizations that promote financial literacy and provide resources to underserved communities.

Creating a legacy of financial empowerment is about more than just accumulating wealth; it's about making a positive impact on the lives of others and the future generations to come. By educating the next generation about money management, engaging in charitable endeavors, and fostering a culture of financial empowerment, we can build a legacy that goes far beyond our personal achievements. Let us embrace this responsibility with enthusiasm and dedication, knowing that our actions today can create a brighter and more financially empowered world for tomorrow.

Chapter 9: Embracing Abundance in All Areas of Life

The Interconnectedness of Abundance in Life

When we think of abundance, the first thing that often comes to mind is financial prosperity. While financial abundance is undoubtedly important, true abundance encompasses much more than just wealth. Abundance is a state of mind and being that extends its reach into all aspects of our lives. In this sub-chapter, we will explore the interconnectedness of abundance in various areas of life and how cultivating abundance in these realms can lead to a richer and more fulfilling existence.

Cultivating Abundance in Relationships and Health

Abundance in relationships goes beyond just the number of friends we have or the size of our social circle. True abundance in relationships stems from the quality of connections we foster and the depth of love and support we share with others. Nurturing meaningful relationships with family, friends, and loved ones brings a sense of joy and belonging that money alone cannot buy.

One of the keys to cultivating abundance in relationships is to practice authentic communication and active listening. By showing genuine interest in others, expressing appreciation, and offering support, we create a positive environment that fosters trust and emotional intimacy. This abundance in relationships not only brings happiness but also a network of people who can uplift and inspire us on our journey towards financial and personal growth.

Furthermore, abundance is deeply connected to our health and well-being. Our bodies are our most valuable asset, and maintaining good health is crucial for living a fulfilling life. When we prioritize self-care through regular exercise, nourishing foods, and sufficient rest, we cultivate abundance in health. A healthy body and mind empower us to pursue our goals with vigor and enthusiasm.

Finding Fulfillment Beyond Material Wealth
While financial abundance can provide comfort and security, it alone cannot bring lasting fulfillment. True fulfillment comes from aligning our actions with our passions and purpose. Pursuing meaningful endeavors, whether it be creative pursuits, philanthropy, or making a positive impact in our community, infuses our lives with a sense of purpose and satisfaction.

When we find fulfillment beyond material wealth, we become less attached to external possessions and more focused on the experiences and memories we create. Engaging in activities that bring joy and meaning into our lives enriches our overall well-being. It allows us to recognize that abundance can be found in the simplest moments, such as spending time with loved ones, enjoying a beautiful sunset, or engaging in acts of kindness.

Balancing Different Aspects of Life for Overall Abundance

The pursuit of abundance requires finding a harmonious balance across all areas of life. Achieving financial success at the expense of our health, relationships, or personal growth can lead to an unbalanced and unfulfilled existence. A holistic approach to abundance involves nurturing all facets of life to create a synergistic effect that enhances our overall well-being.

Practicing time management and setting priorities can help us strike a balance between our personal and professional commitments. By establishing boundaries and allocating time for self-care, relationships, and pursuing our passions, we create space for abundance to flourish. This balanced approach empowers us to excel in our financial endeavors while fostering a fulfilling and meaningful life.

Abundance in life extends far beyond financial prosperity. It encompasses cultivating meaningful relationships, prioritizing our health and well-being, and finding fulfillment beyond material possessions. When we embrace abundance in all areas of life and create a harmonious balance, we unlock the true potential for a rich and fulfilling existence. As we journey towards financial success, let us also remember to cherish the interconnectedness of abundance in every aspect of our lives.

Remember, true abundance is not a destination but a way of life, and by living with a mindset of abundance, we attract even greater prosperity in all its forms.

Aligning Your Values with Financial Choices

When you understand how your money choices reflect your core beliefs, you'll be better equipped to make conscious and purposeful financial decisions that align with your true desires and aspirations. By integrating your values into your financial choices, you can create a life of abundance that extends far beyond monetary wealth.

Integrating Personal Values into Money Decisions

Our values are the guiding principles that shape our beliefs and behaviors. When it comes to money, understanding and integrating your personal values can significantly impact your financial well-being. Take a moment to reflect on what truly matters to you in life. Is it family, adventure, education, community, or personal growth? Identifying your core values is a crucial first step towards aligning your financial choices with your heart's desires.

Prioritizing Spending According to Values

Once you've identified your core values, it's time to prioritize your spending accordingly. Allocate your financial resources to areas that hold significant meaning to you. For example, if you value experiences and travel, you might decide to spend more on trips and adventures rather than on material possessions. On the other hand, if family is your top priority, you might allocate funds to create lasting memories and experiences with your loved ones.

Assessing Your Financial Goals

As you align your values with your financial choices, it's essential to review your financial goals regularly. Ensure that your objectives are in harmony with your values and not driven solely by external pressures or societal norms. By connecting your aspirations to your values, you'll find greater motivation and fulfillment in pursuing your financial objectives.

Conscious Consumption and Sustainable Spending
In today's world, mindful consumption is gaining popularity as people seek to make more conscious choices that benefit both themselves and the planet. Conscious consumption involves being aware of the impact of your purchases on the environment, society, and your well-being. Here's how you can embrace sustainable spending and conscious consumption:

Prioritize Quality Over Quantity

Instead of mindlessly accumulating possessions, focus on acquiring high-quality items that are durable and serve a meaningful purpose in your life. Investing in well-made products might involve a higher initial cost, but their longevity and satisfaction will make them more valuable in the long run.

Support Ethical and Sustainable Brands

Align your spending with companies that prioritize ethical practices, environmental sustainability, and social responsibility. Look for businesses that promote fair wages, eco-friendly manufacturing processes, and giving back to the community.

Reduce Waste and Reuse

Take steps to minimize waste and embrace a culture of reuse. Opt for reusable products and reduce single-use items in your daily life. Not only will this save you money in the long term, but it will also contribute to a healthier planet.

Investing in Experiences and Personal Growth

While material possessions can provide temporary happiness, experiences and personal growth are lasting sources of joy and abundance. When you invest in experiences and self-improvement, you create memories and develop skills that enrich your life in meaningful ways.

Prioritize Experiences Over Material Things

Experiences have the power to create lasting happiness and fulfillment. Consider allocating a portion of your budget to travel, cultural events, or learning opportunities that align with your interests and passions.

Invest in Your Education and Skills

Personal growth is an investment in yourself that pays dividends throughout your life. Whether it's further education, skill development, or pursuing a new hobby, investing in yourself can open doors to new opportunities and enhance your financial potential.

Cultivate a Growth Mindset

A growth mindset is essential for embracing abundance in all areas of life. Embrace challenges and view them as opportunities for learning and growth. With a growth mindset, setbacks become stepping stones, and you become more resilient in your pursuit of financial success.

Aligning your values with your financial choices is a powerful way to embrace abundance in all areas of life. By integrating your personal values into money decisions, you'll experience a deeper sense of purpose, fulfillment, and financial well-being. Conscious consumption and sustainable spending not only benefit you but also contribute to a healthier planet and society. Investing in experiences and personal growth enriches your life and provides lasting happiness beyond material possessions. Remember, your financial choices are a reflection of your values, and by making intentional and purposeful decisions, you can create a life of true abundance.

The Power of Gratitude and Contentment

True abundance extends far beyond financial success. It lies in cultivating a mindset of gratitude and contentment, where we appreciate the blessings we have while still striving for growth and prosperity. In this sub-chapter, we will explore how practicing gratitude can lead to true abundance and how embracing contentment enriches our lives on a profound level.

Practicing Gratitude as a Path to True Abundance

Gratitude is a transformative force that has the power to shift our focus from what we lack to what we already have. It is a simple yet profound practice that can open the floodgates to abundance in all aspects of life. When we express genuine gratitude for our blessings, we create a positive energy that attracts more goodness into our lives.

To practice gratitude, start by setting aside a few minutes each day to reflect on the things you are thankful for. It could be something as small as a warm cup of coffee in the morning or a kind word from a friend. By acknowledging these moments of grace, we become more attuned to the abundance that surrounds us.

An attitude of gratitude also helps us build resilience during challenging times. Instead of dwelling on what's missing or what went wrong, we shift our focus to the lessons we've learned and the strength we've gained from overcoming obstacles. This positive mindset allows us to approach future challenges with a sense of optimism and confidence.

Embracing Contentment While Aspiring for Financial Growth

Contentment should not be confused with complacency; rather, it is about finding peace and satisfaction in the present moment while still pursuing our goals. Many people fall into the trap of constantly seeking more, believing that happiness lies in the next achievement or acquisition. However, this perpetual cycle of desire can lead to perpetual dissatisfaction.

Contentment, on the other hand, is the ability to appreciate what we have achieved and acquired without diminishing our ambitions. It allows us to savor the journey towards our financial goals, rather than fixating solely on the destination. When we embrace contentment, we release the pressure of always needing more and allow ourselves to experience joy and fulfillment in the present.

Of course, this doesn't mean we should abandon our aspirations or settle for mediocrity. Instead, contentment acts as a foundation for growth. By acknowledging our progress and celebrating our achievements, we fuel our motivation to keep striving for greater financial abundance.

Living in the Present Moment for Lasting Happiness

The present moment is the only reality we truly have, yet we often find ourselves dwelling on the past or anxiously anticipating the future. The key to lasting happiness and abundance is to embrace the present moment fully.

Mindfulness is a practice that enables us to be fully present and engaged in each moment of our lives. When we cultivate mindfulness, we become attuned to the beauty and opportunities that surround us every day. This heightened awareness helps us recognize the abundance that exists in simple pleasures and everyday experiences.

Moreover, living in the present moment allows us to make conscious choices that align with our values and aspirations. It keeps us from getting carried away by impulsive decisions driven by external pressures or societal expectations. By staying anchored in the now, we can make wise financial decisions that support our long-term goals and well-being.

The power of gratitude and contentment cannot be overstated. When we practice gratitude, we attract more blessings and positive experiences into our lives. Embracing contentment allows us to find fulfillment in our current circumstances while maintaining our drive for financial growth. And by living in the present moment, we open ourselves up to a world of abundance and joy that exists right here, right now. So, let's embark on this journey of embracing abundance in all areas of life, starting with a grateful heart and a contented spirit.

Chapter 10: Overcoming Money Fears and Challenges

Identifying and Addressing Money Fears

Money, a topic that evokes various emotions within us - excitement, anxiety, and sometimes even fear. The fear of money, also known as financial fear, is a common experience shared by many. It can stem from various sources, including past experiences, societal conditioning, and personal beliefs. In this chapter, we will explore some common money fears, understand their origins, and equip ourselves with powerful techniques to confront and overcome these fears. By doing so, we can find the courage and confidence to pursue our financial goals and create a more abundant future.

Common Money Fears and Their Origins

a) Fear of Scarcity: One of the most prevalent money fears is the fear of scarcity - the belief that there will never be enough money to meet one's needs and desires. This fear often has its roots in childhood experiences, such as growing up in a financially unstable environment or witnessing financial struggles within the family. These early experiences can leave a lasting impression on our subconscious mind, leading us to view money as something scarce and unattainable.

b) Fear of Failure: Many individuals fear making financial decisions or taking risks due to the fear of failure. This fear can manifest as procrastination or avoiding opportunities that have the potential for financial growth. It often results from past experiences of financial setbacks or witnessing others facing financial challenges. The fear of failure can hinder our willingness to invest, start a business, or pursue new career opportunities.

c) Fear of Success: Surprisingly, the fear of success is another common money fear. This fear arises from a fear of change and the unknown that comes with financial success. It may involve worries about managing newfound wealth, handling increased responsibilities, or facing envy and criticism from others. As a result, some individuals unconsciously sabotage their own financial progress to remain within their comfort zone.

d) Fear of Judgement: The fear of being judged based on one's financial situation can be paralyzing. It often stems from societal pressures and expectations around money and material possessions. The fear of judgment can lead to feelings of inadequacy and unworthiness, preventing individuals from taking positive financial actions and seeking help when needed.

Techniques to Confront and Overcome Money Fears
a) Awareness and Acceptance: The first step in overcoming money fears is to become aware of them and acknowledge their presence in our lives. Reflect on your beliefs and emotions about money and identify any patterns of fear or anxiety. Once you acknowledge these fears, remember that it's normal to experience them, and it doesn't define your worth or capabilities.

b) Challenging Negative Beliefs: To counteract money fears, challenge the negative beliefs associated with them. Replace thoughts like "I'll never have enough money" with more empowering beliefs such as "I am capable of attracting abundance." Write down these positive affirmations and repeat them daily to reinforce your new mindset.

c) Education and Knowledge: Often, money fears arise from a lack of financial literacy and understanding. Educate yourself about personal finance, investment strategies, and money management. Knowledge is a powerful tool that can boost your confidence and help you make informed financial decisions.

d) Visualization and Positive Reinforcement: Use visualization techniques to see yourself overcoming financial challenges and achieving your goals. Imagine yourself living a life of abundance and financial freedom. Visualize the steps you take to confront money fears and the positive outcomes that result from your actions.

e) Seek Support: Don't be afraid to seek support from friends, family, or financial advisors. Talking openly about your money fears can help you gain perspective and receive valuable insights from others who may have experienced similar challenges.

Finding Courage and Confidence in Financial Pursuits
a) Taking Small Steps: Overcoming money fears doesn't require taking giant leaps. Start by taking small steps

towards your financial goals. Celebrate each achievement, no matter how insignificant it may seem. Each step forward builds momentum and confidence.

b) Embracing Failure as a Learning Opportunity: Remember that failure is a natural part of any journey, including your financial one. Embrace failures as valuable learning opportunities that pave the way for growth and improvement.

c) Cultivating a Growth Mindset: Adopt a growth mindset that thrives on challenges and sees effort as a path to mastery. Embrace a willingness to learn, adapt, and grow, knowing that setbacks are stepping stones to success.

d) Celebrating Progress: Celebrate your progress, both big and small. Acknowledge the courage it takes to face money fears and take proactive steps towards a more abundant future.

Identifying and addressing money fears is a crucial step towards achieving financial empowerment and abundance. By recognizing the common money fears and their origins, and employing various techniques to confront and overcome them, we can build the courage and confidence needed to pursue our financial dreams. Remember that fear is a natural human emotion, but it doesn't have to dictate your financial journey. Embrace the process of growth, learning, and resilience as you move towards a life of financial well-being and abundance. You've got this!

Navigating Through Economic Ups and Downs

In life, financial uncertainty is an inevitable reality. Economic ups and downs, market fluctuations, and unexpected events can all pose challenges to our financial stability. However, by developing resilience and implementing smart strategies, we can not only survive but also thrive during economic downturns. In this section, we will explore how to navigate through economic ups and downs, build resilience in times of financial uncertainty, and create an emergency financial plan to safeguard our financial well-being.

Developing Resilience in Times of Financial Uncertainty

When faced with financial uncertainty, our ability to bounce back and adapt is crucial. Developing resilience allows us to remain strong, focused, and confident during challenging times. Here are some key points to consider when building resilience:

1. Stay Positive and Proactive: Maintaining a positive attitude and taking proactive steps to address financial challenges is vital. Rather than dwelling on the negative, focus on what you can control and take action to improve your situation.

2. Build a Strong Support System: Surround yourself with supportive friends, family, or mentors who can provide guidance and encouragement. Sharing concerns and seeking advice can lighten the emotional burden and help you gain valuable insights.

3. Diversify Your Income Streams: Relying on a single source of income can leave you vulnerable to economic downturns. Consider diversifying your income streams through side hustles, investments, or passive income sources to create a more stable financial foundation.

4. Maintain a Long-Term Perspective: Economic fluctuations are a natural part of the financial cycle. Remember that downturns are often followed by periods of growth. Keeping a long-term perspective can help you weather short-term challenges more effectively.

Strategies for Surviving and Thriving in Economic Downturns

Economic downturns can be daunting, but they also present opportunities for growth and learning. By adopting effective strategies, you can not only survive but also thrive during these challenging times. Consider the following approaches:

1. Create a Financial Contingency Plan: Review your financial situation and create a contingency plan to address potential income reductions or job losses. Having a clear plan in place can alleviate anxiety and provide a roadmap during uncertain times.

2. Cut Unnecessary Expenses: Evaluate your expenses and identify areas where you can cut back without sacrificing essential needs. Prioritize spending on necessities and reduce discretionary expenses until your financial situation stabilizes.

3. Focus on Debt Repayment: Reducing debt during economic downturns can significantly improve your financial security. Prioritize high-interest debts and consider refinancing options to lower interest rates.

4. Invest Wisely: While market volatility can be intimidating, it can also present opportunities for strategic investments. Consider working with a financial advisor to identify undervalued assets or investment options that align with your risk tolerance and financial goals.

Building an Emergency Financial Plan
Having an emergency financial plan in place is like building a safety net to protect yourself and your loved ones during challenging times. Here's how to create a robust emergency financial plan:

1. Assess Your Current Financial Situation: Start by evaluating your current financial standing, including assets, liabilities, and available savings. Understanding your financial position is essential in crafting an effective emergency plan.

2. Establish an Emergency Fund: Aim to save three to six months' worth of living expenses in an easily accessible savings account. This fund will serve as a financial buffer during unexpected events, such as job loss or medical emergencies.

3. Review and Update Insurance Coverage: Ensure that you have adequate insurance coverage, including health, life, and property insurance. Having the right policies in place can protect you from significant financial burdens in times of crisis.

4. Create a Budget for Hard Times: Develop a budget that outlines essential expenses and discretionary spending. This will help you prioritize financial decisions and make necessary adjustments during economic downturns.

5. Explore Government Assistance Programs: Familiarize yourself with available government assistance programs that can provide support during financial hardships. Research eligibility criteria and application procedures to be prepared if the need arises.

Remember that while economic uncertainty is part of life, your preparedness and mindset will play a significant role in shaping your financial well-being. Stay positive, stay informed, and take control of your financial future.

Seeking Support and Guidance for Financial Well-being

In our journey towards financial prosperity, it's not uncommon to encounter challenges and fears that can make the path ahead seem daunting. However, the good news is that you don't have to face these obstacles alone. Seeking support and guidance from the right sources can be instrumental in helping you navigate through financial uncertainties and emerge stronger on the other side. In this section, we will explore the various ways you can seek support and surround yourself with a network of people who can contribute to your financial well-being.

The Role of Financial Advisors and Mentors

A trusted financial advisor or mentor can be an invaluable asset on your path to financial success. These professionals possess a wealth of knowledge and experience in handling various financial situations and can provide personalized guidance based on your unique circumstances. Whether you are just starting your journey or looking to grow your wealth, a financial advisor can assist you in setting clear financial goals, creating a comprehensive financial plan, and making informed investment decisions.

Mentors, on the other hand, are experienced individuals who have walked a similar path and can offer valuable insights and advice from their own experiences. They can share their successes and failures, helping you avoid common pitfalls and make informed choices. A mentor can be someone you know personally, a colleague, or even someone you admire from afar, as long as they are willing to guide you on your financial journey.

When choosing a financial advisor or mentor, it's crucial to find someone who aligns with your values and understands your financial objectives. Establishing a strong rapport and open communication with them will ensure that you get the most out of their guidance.

Joining Supportive Financial Communities

The saying, "You are the average of the five people you spend the most time with," holds true even in the realm of finances. Being part of a supportive financial community can significantly impact your financial mindset and behavior. Such communities can provide a safe space to share experiences, ask questions, and receive encouragement from like-minded individuals who are also on their journey to financial abundance.

You can find supportive financial communities in various forms, from local investment clubs to online forums and social media groups. These communities offer an opportunity to engage in discussions about financial strategies, investment opportunities, and money management tips. Additionally, they can serve as a source of motivation during challenging times and help you stay focused on your financial goals.

Balancing Independence with Seeking Help When Needed

While it's essential to take ownership of your financial journey, there may be instances where seeking help is necessary. Balancing independence with knowing when to ask for assistance is a sign of wisdom and maturity in managing your finances.

It's natural to want to handle everything on your own, but some financial matters can be complex and require expert advice. For example, tax planning, estate planning, or starting a business may call for specialized knowledge that you may not possess. In such cases, seeking the counsel of professionals in these fields can save you time, money, and potential mistakes.

To maintain independence while seeking help, take an active role in your financial decisions. Ask questions, understand the recommendations given, and ensure that they align with your financial objectives. Being proactive in your approach will empower you to make informed choices while benefitting from expert advice.

Seeking support and guidance for your financial well-being is a smart and proactive approach to overcoming money fears and challenges. By surrounding yourself with trusted financial advisors, mentors, and supportive communities, you can gain the knowledge, insights, and motivation needed to navigate through uncertain times. Additionally, striking a balance between independence and seeking help when needed will empower you to make sound financial decisions and ultimately achieve your goals.

You are not alone on this journey; there are resources and people ready to support you. Embrace the guidance available to you, learn from others' experiences, and continue your pursuit of financial success with confidence and determination.

Chapter 11: Embracing Lifelong Learning and Growth

The Connection Between Learning and Financial Success

In the pursuit of financial success and abundance, one of the most powerful tools at your disposal is continuous learning. The journey to building wealth is not a destination but a dynamic process that requires adaptability, perseverance, and a hunger for knowledge. In this sub-chapter, we will explore the undeniable connection between learning and financial success and uncover how investing in personal development can significantly impact your path to prosperity. Moreover, we'll discuss the importance of evolving with the ever-changing financial landscape to stay ahead in your financial endeavors.

The Power of Continuous Learning in Wealth Building

Imagine your mind as a vast ocean, capable of receiving, processing, and implementing new ideas and strategies. When it comes to wealth building, continuous learning is akin to the lifeblood that keeps your financial journey flowing. Embracing a growth mindset and actively seeking opportunities to learn, whether through books, seminars, workshops, or online courses, can set you apart on your journey to financial prosperity.

Continuous learning in the realm of wealth building serves several purposes. Firstly, it empowers you with knowledge about various investment opportunities and financial instruments. As you deepen your understanding of the financial markets, you gain the confidence to make informed decisions that align with your financial goals. Secondly, it helps you identify and seize opportunities that others may overlook. The world of finance is ever-evolving, and staying updated allows you to stay one step ahead of the curve.

Furthermore, continuous learning is a crucial component in managing risks effectively. Financial markets can be unpredictable, and by keeping yourself informed and educated, you can make proactive decisions to safeguard your wealth during turbulent times. Remember, knowledge is not static, and continuous learning allows you to refine and expand your financial strategies as you grow.

Investing in Personal Development for Financial Growth
It is said that your greatest asset is not the money in your bank account but the person you become. Personal development goes hand in hand with financial growth, as your mindset, habits, and skills play a pivotal role in shaping your financial outcomes.

One key aspect of personal development is developing a strong money mindset. Your beliefs about money can either propel you forward or hold you back. By investing time and effort into understanding and transforming your money beliefs, you pave the way for a healthier relationship with money. Positive money beliefs encourage you to attract wealth and abundance into your life.

Moreover, personal development encompasses honing essential financial skills, such as budgeting, saving, and investing. These skills are the building blocks of financial success and stability. Taking the initiative to learn and improve these skills not only helps you achieve your financial goals but also empowers you to weather financial challenges with confidence.

Beyond financial skills, personal development includes enhancing your emotional intelligence, communication abilities, and leadership qualities. These attributes play a significant role in building successful businesses, negotiating lucrative deals, and networking effectively. As you invest in your personal development, you become better equipped to seize opportunities and navigate the complexities of the financial world.

Evolving with the Changing Financial Landscape
The financial landscape is in a constant state of flux. From advancements in technology to shifts in global markets, the world of finance is continuously evolving. To thrive in this dynamic environment, adaptability is key.

As you embrace lifelong learning, it becomes easier to stay attuned to changes in the financial landscape. The ability to adapt and stay ahead of emerging trends is what separates successful wealth builders from those who struggle to keep up.

For instance, consider the rise of cryptocurrencies. A decade ago, cryptocurrencies like Bitcoin were virtually unheard of, but they have now become a significant player in the financial world. Those who recognized the potential of this emerging asset class early on were able to capitalize on its growth.

Being open to new opportunities and technologies can lead to innovative investment strategies and business ventures. However, while embracing change is essential, it is equally vital to approach new opportunities with caution. Continuously learning about new investment options and seeking advice from reputable financial experts can help you navigate through potential risks and make informed decisions.

The connection between learning and financial success is undeniable. Continuous learning fuels your financial journey, equipping you with knowledge, skills, and the right mindset to prosper. Investing in personal development complements your financial growth, empowering you to become the best version of yourself and attract abundance into your life. Finally, staying adaptable and evolving with the ever-changing financial landscape ensures that you are well-positioned to seize opportunities and overcome challenges on your path to enduring wealth. Embrace the power of learning and unlock the boundless potential for financial success that lies within you.

Pursuing Passion Projects and Side Ventures
Embracing lifelong learning and growth is a key ingredient in the recipe for success, and passion projects and side ventures can play a significant role in shaping your financial future.

The Role of Passion in Finding Financial Opportunities
Passion is like a guiding star that leads us towards our true purpose and fulfillment. When you align your financial goals with your passions, remarkable things can happen. Many successful entrepreneurs and individuals attribute their achievements to their unwavering passion for what they do.

When you pursue projects that genuinely ignite your enthusiasm, you are more likely to invest your time and energy wholeheartedly. This dedication often leads to a higher level of expertise and skill development, setting you apart from others in the field. Moreover, your passion will shine through your work, attracting like-minded individuals who share your enthusiasm and creating a supportive community around your endeavors.

Remember, passion is not solely limited to specific industries or professions. It can be found in various activities and hobbies. So, take a moment to reflect on what truly excites you, as this will be the cornerstone of your financial opportunities.

Balancing Stability and Risk in Side Ventures

While passion is essential, it's equally crucial to balance stability and risk when exploring side ventures. Side ventures are endeavors pursued alongside your primary source of income, which can provide diversification and financial security.

It's natural to be eager to dive headfirst into your passion projects, but consider the financial implications and the risks involved. Start by assessing your current financial situation, including your income, expenses, and savings. Ensure that you have a solid financial foundation to support your side ventures.

It's prudent to strike a balance between your main income source and your side ventures. While side ventures can be exciting and potentially lucrative, they may take time to gain traction. Be realistic about the time and effort you can allocate to your projects while maintaining stability in your primary income stream.

Strategies for Turning Hobbies into Profitable Ventures

Transforming hobbies into profitable ventures is a fulfilling way to combine passion with financial gain. Whether you love baking, photography, crafting, or playing a musical instrument, there are opportunities to monetize your hobbies.

1. Identify Your Niche: Determine what makes your hobby unique and how it can solve a problem or fulfill a need in the market. Understanding your niche will help you target the right audience and tailor your offerings accordingly.

2. Market Research: Conduct thorough market research to assess demand and competition in your chosen niche. Identify gaps in the market that align with your hobby, giving you a competitive advantage.

3. Create a Business Plan: Treat your hobby-turned-venture as a business. Develop a comprehensive business plan that outlines your goals, target audience, marketing strategies, and financial projections.

4. Build Your Brand: Establish a strong brand identity that reflects your passion and resonates with your target audience. Your brand should convey the essence of your hobby and what sets it apart.

5. Start Small and Grow: Begin by offering your products or services on a small scale. Use feedback from early customers to refine and improve your offerings. As your venture gains traction, gradually expand your reach.

6. Utilize Online Platforms: Leverage the power of online platforms to reach a wider audience. Social media, e-commerce websites, and online marketplaces can be invaluable tools for showcasing your creations and attracting customers.

7. Network and Collaborate: Connect with like-minded individuals and potential collaborators in your industry. Collaborations can introduce your venture to new audiences and provide opportunities for mutual growth.

8. Customer Engagement: Engage with your customers actively and build a loyal community around your venture. Offer exceptional customer service, seek feedback, and respond to queries promptly.

9. Adapt and Innovate: Stay adaptable to changing market trends and customer preferences. Continuously innovate your offerings to keep them fresh and appealing.

Turning your hobby into a profitable venture may not happen overnight, and that's okay. It's a journey of learning, growth, and perseverance. Keep nurturing your passion, stay open to learning, and be resilient in the face of challenges.

Pursuing passion projects and side ventures is a wonderful way to blend your interests with financial opportunities. Let your passion be your driving force, but remember to strike a balance between stability and risk. With dedication, creativity, and a willingness to learn, you can turn your hobbies into profitable and fulfilling ventures. So, go ahead, embrace your passion, and let it lead you on a path of both personal and financial growth.

The Art of Adaptation and Resilience

In our journey to best friends with money, we come to understand that the road to financial success is not always smooth and straightforward. Life is full of surprises, both positive and challenging, and it's essential to embrace the art of adaptation and resilience to navigate through the ever-evolving landscape of finance. In this sub-chapter, we will explore how flexibility in financial planning, thriving in evolving economic conditions, and learning from setbacks can become stepping stones towards greater financial abundance and security.

Embracing Flexibility in Financial Planning

Financial planning is the foundation of sound money management, but it should not be a rigid set of rules. The key to sustainable financial planning is to be flexible and adaptable to changing circumstances. Life is unpredictable, and what may have worked for you a few years ago may not be suitable for your current situation.

As you embark on your financial journey, be open to reassessing and adjusting your financial plans regularly. This could involve reviewing your budget to accommodate new expenses or shifting your investment strategies based on market conditions. By embracing flexibility, you can make informed decisions that align with your current goals and aspirations.

Furthermore, consider setting aside an emergency fund to serve as a buffer during unexpected financial challenges. Having this safety net provides peace of mind, knowing that you can handle unforeseen circumstances without derailing your long-term financial objectives.

Thriving in Evolving Economic Conditions

The financial world is in constant flux, with economic conditions fluctuating due to various factors such as global events, technological advancements, and market trends. Thriving in such an environment requires adaptability and a proactive mindset.

Stay informed about economic trends and developments through reputable sources and financial experts. Knowledge is a powerful tool, and understanding the implications of economic changes can help you make strategic financial decisions. Keep an eye on industries and sectors that show promise and align with your interests or expertise.

Moreover, diversify your investment portfolio to spread risk across various assets. A well-diversified portfolio is more likely to withstand economic downturns, as not all investments will be affected in the same way. This way, you can mitigate losses in one area with gains in another.

Learning from Setbacks and Using Them as Stepping Stones

Setbacks are a natural part of any journey, including the path to financial success. Rather than viewing setbacks as failures, see them as valuable learning experiences. Each setback provides an opportunity to grow, adapt, and come back stronger.

When facing financial challenges, take the time to reflect on what went wrong and identify areas for improvement. Use these insights to refine your strategies and avoid making the same mistakes in the future. Seek advice from financial mentors or experts to gain fresh perspectives and guidance.

Remember that setbacks are not a reflection of your worth or abilities. Treat them as temporary roadblocks on your path to financial abundance. Stay persistent and remain focused on your long-term goals. By maintaining a growth mindset, setbacks can become stepping stones that propel you forward rather than obstacles that hold you back.

The art of adaptation and resilience plays a crucial role in our journey to becoming best friends with money. Embracing flexibility in financial planning, thriving in evolving economic conditions, and learning from setbacks are all essential components of this art. By being open to change, staying informed, and using setbacks as opportunities for growth, you can build a solid foundation for financial success and abundance in your life. Remember that lifelong learning and growth are not just limited to finances; they extend to all areas of life, contributing to a fulfilling and prosperous journey overall.

Chapter 12: Sustaining the Money Mindset

Integrating the Money Mindset as a Way of Life

Congratulations! You've come a long way on your journey to transform your relationship with money and embrace the abundant life you deserve. By now, you've learned the ins and outs of attracting money, setting clear financial goals, and developing healthy money habits. However, the real magic lies in sustaining this newfound money mindset for the long term. In this sub-chapter, we'll explore how to make the money mindset an integral part of your life, ensuring that it becomes a habit, creating a supportive environment to reinforce your mindset, and celebrating your financial journey and achievements.

Making the Money Mindset a Habit

They say that success is the sum of small efforts repeated day in and day out. This notion holds true for adopting a money mindset as well. The key to making the money mindset a habit is consistency. Like any other habit, it requires practice and dedication, but fear not, it's easier than you might think.

1. Morning Affirmations: Start your day on the right foot by incorporating positive money affirmations into your morning routine. Remind yourself that you are deserving of financial abundance and that money flows to you effortlessly. Repeat these affirmations with conviction and believe in their truth.

2. Visualization: Take a few minutes each day to visualize your financial goals. Imagine yourself achieving them, feel the excitement, and immerse yourself in the emotions of success. Visualization creates a powerful connection between your mind and your goals, reinforcing the money mindset.

3. Consistent Learning: Keep learning about money and finance. Attend seminars, read books, and listen to podcasts that align with your financial goals. The more you educate yourself about money matters, the better equipped you'll be to sustain your money mindset.

4. Gratitude Journaling: Cultivate an attitude of gratitude towards your financial journey. Write down at least three things you're grateful for each day, whether it's a small financial win or the abundance you already have. Gratitude shifts your focus from lack to abundance, nurturing the money mindset.

Cultivating a Supportive Environment for Your Mindset
They say, "You are the average of the five people you spend the most time with." Surrounding yourself with a supportive environment can significantly impact your ability to sustain the money mindset. Here's how to create an environment that nurtures your financial growth:

1. Positive Money Conversations: Engage in positive and constructive discussions about money with friends, family, or like-minded individuals. Share your goals and aspirations, and be open to receiving and giving financial advice.

2. Limiting Negative Influences: Identify negative influences that might discourage your money mindset. Whether it's media portraying scarcity or friends with a pessimistic outlook on finances, limit your exposure to such influences.

3. Mastermind Groups: Consider joining a mastermind group or financial support network. These groups provide accountability, encouragement, and a space to share experiences and challenges.

4. Find a Money Mentor: Look for someone who has successfully adopted a money mindset and is willing to mentor you. Learning from their experiences and insights can be invaluable on your own financial journey.

Celebrating Your Financial Journey and Achievements
In the pursuit of financial abundance, it's essential to celebrate every milestone and achievement, no matter how big or small. Celebrating your successes not only boosts your confidence but also reinforces the positive neural pathways associated with your money mindset.

1. Set Milestone Rewards: Create a system of rewards for yourself whenever you achieve a financial goal or reach a milestone. Treat yourself to something you enjoy or invest in an experience that brings you joy.

2. Track Your Progress: Keep a journal of your financial journey, noting down your accomplishments and challenges along the way. Reflect on how far you've come and how much you've grown.

3. Practice Gratefulness: Express gratitude for the abundance in your life, including the financial gains. Gratefulness further strengthens your money mindset and attracts more positive experiences.

4. Share Your Successes: Share your financial victories with those who have supported you on your journey. Your achievements will inspire others to embrace their money mindset and attract abundance as well.

Sustaining the money mindset is not about being perfect or never encountering challenges. It's about resilience and staying committed to your growth. By making the money mindset a habit, surrounding yourself with a supportive environment, and celebrating your progress, you will undoubtedly continue to attract and embrace abundance in your life. Keep going, and your financial dreams will be well within your grasp.

Maintaining Balance and Well-being in Wealth Accumulation

You've come a long way on your journey towards cultivating a healthy money mindset and attracting abundance into your life. Now, as you continue on this path, it's crucial to understand how to sustain your progress and ensure that wealth accumulation doesn't come at the cost of your well-being. In this section, we will explore the vital connection between wealth and well-being, offer insights into avoiding the trap of constant financial obsession, and provide practical tips for practicing self-care and mindfulness alongside your financial goals.

The Connection Between Wealth and Well-being
As you work towards building and sustaining wealth, it's essential to recognize that true prosperity extends beyond mere financial gains. While money can undoubtedly provide a sense of security and open doors to various opportunities, it's equally crucial to nurture your overall well-being. A holistic approach to wealth includes physical, emotional, and mental well-being.

Studies have shown that there is a strong correlation between financial well-being and overall life satisfaction. However, it's crucial to strike a balance and not let your pursuit of financial goals consume every aspect of your life. Taking care of your health, nurturing meaningful relationships, and finding time for hobbies and passions are equally important in maintaining a fulfilling life.

Avoiding the Trap of Constant Financial Obsession
In today's fast-paced and materialistic world, it's easy to fall into the trap of constant financial obsession. While it's natural to be enthusiastic about your financial goals and

future prospects, becoming overly fixated on money can have adverse effects on your mental health and relationships.

The fear of losing wealth, comparing oneself to others, and chasing material possessions can create unnecessary stress and anxiety. It's crucial to recognize that money is a tool to enhance your life, not the sole measure of your self-worth or success. Instead of obsessing over every penny, focus on making sound financial decisions and trust in your abilities to navigate through challenges.

Practicing Self-Care and Mindfulness Alongside Financial Goals

To ensure that wealth accumulation doesn't compromise your well-being, incorporating self-care and mindfulness practices into your daily routine is essential. Self-care involves nurturing your physical, emotional, and mental health, while mindfulness allows you to stay present and aware of your thoughts and feelings.

1. Physical Well-being:

Prioritize your physical health by engaging in regular exercise, maintaining a balanced diet, and getting enough restful sleep. A healthy body provides the energy and focus needed to pursue your financial goals effectively.

2. Emotional Well-being:

Acknowledge and process your emotions surrounding money. Cultivate a positive relationship with money by celebrating your achievements and learning from setbacks. Seek support from loved ones or a financial advisor when needed.

3. Mental Well-being:

Stay mentally sharp by engaging in activities that challenge your mind, such as reading, puzzles, or learning new skills. Limit exposure to negative financial news that may trigger anxiety or fear.

4. Mindfulness Practices:

Incorporate mindfulness practices like meditation, deep breathing, or journaling into your daily routine. These practices help reduce stress, increase self-awareness, and provide clarity in decision-making.

5. Time for Joy and Play:

Make time for activities that bring you joy and fulfillment. Engage in hobbies, spend quality time with loved ones, or pursue creative outlets. Remember, life is about more than just money; it's about finding meaning and happiness in every moment.

As you continue on your journey, remember that true wealth encompasses not only the dollars in your bank account but also the richness of your experiences, relationships, and personal growth. Be kind to yourself, stay focused on your goals, and above all, cherish the journey towards a life of abundance and well-being. You've got this!

Leaving a Legacy of Abundance

In the journey of mastering the art of attracting and keeping money, it is not just about personal financial success; it is also about leaving a lasting impact beyond our own lifetime. As you continue to embrace the money mindset and enjoy the fruits of your efforts, it becomes essential to think about how you can leave a legacy of abundance that extends far beyond your years. This section delves into the importance of creating a positive impact beyond your lifetime, educating future generations on the money mindset, and inspiring others to attract abundance in their lives.

Creating a Positive Impact Beyond Your Lifetime

One of the most powerful ways to sustain the money mindset is to think beyond your immediate desires and consider how your wealth can be a force for good in the world. A legacy of abundance goes beyond amassing wealth; it involves using that wealth to make a positive impact on the lives of others and contributing to causes that are meaningful to you.

Consider engaging in philanthropy and charitable activities that align with your values and passions. Whether it's supporting educational initiatives, environmental conservation efforts, or social entrepreneurship, your financial resources can create a ripple effect of positive change. Remember that giving back not only benefits others but also brings a sense of fulfillment and purpose to your own life.

Take the time to identify causes that resonate with you deeply. Get involved personally by volunteering or actively participating in initiatives that your wealth can support. By doing so, you create a meaningful connection between your money and your values, reinforcing the abundance mindset and ensuring a lasting legacy of positive impact.

Educating Future Generations on Money Mindset
Passing down financial knowledge and a positive money mindset to future generations is a gift that keeps on giving. As you continue your journey of attracting and staying best friends with money, consider the impact of educating your children, grandchildren, or even the wider community about financial literacy and abundance.

Children often learn from the behaviors and attitudes of their parents and role models. By openly discussing money matters, teaching the importance of saving and investing, and demonstrating responsible financial habits, you lay the foundation for a healthy relationship with money in the next generation.

Additionally, consider involving your family in financial decision-making. Provide opportunities for them to learn about budgeting, setting financial goals, and making informed investment choices. Instilling a sense of financial responsibility and empowerment early on can lead to a more secure financial future for your loved ones.

Inspiring Others to Attract Abundance in Their Lives

As you continue to cultivate a money mindset that attracts wealth and abundance, your own journey becomes an inspiration for others. Share your experiences, successes, and challenges with those around you. Your story can motivate and empower others to embark on their own path to financial prosperity.

Remember that inspiring others does not always require grand gestures or significant wealth. Simple acts of kindness, generosity, and sharing valuable insights can have a profound impact on someone's life. Engage in discussions about money openly and positively, breaking the taboo surrounding financial matters.

Furthermore, consider mentoring or supporting individuals who are eager to improve their financial situation. Your guidance and encouragement can be a transformative force in helping them change their money mindset and achieve greater financial stability.

Sustaining the money mindset goes beyond personal gain; it involves leaving a legacy of abundance that extends to the lives of others and future generations. By creating a positive impact through philanthropy, educating others on financial literacy, and inspiring individuals to attract abundance, you build a legacy that transcends time and influences the world for the better. Remember that true abundance is not solely about wealth; it's about the positive and meaningful imprint you leave on the lives of others. As you continue on your journey, may your money mindset be

a beacon of hope, empowerment, and abundance for all
those whose lives you touch.

Conclusion

Congratulations on reaching the end of this transformative journey! Throughout this book, we've explored the untold secrets to attracting money and keeping it beside you. We've delved into the power of the money mindset, setting clear financial goals, creating multiple streams of income, and mastering the art of budgeting and saving. We've learned to cultivate healthy money habits, overcome money fears and challenges, and even leave a legacy of abundance that extends far beyond our own lifetimes.

Now, as we conclude, let's take a moment to reflect on the essence of money and how it can truly become your best friend. Money, at its core, is not just a mere means of exchange; it is a reflection of your thoughts, beliefs, and actions. It is a mirror that reflects your relationship with abundance and your capacity to manifest the life you desire. When you embrace money as your ally rather than your adversary, you open the floodgates of prosperity and limitless possibilities.

A Fresh Perspective on Money

To deeply understand money, you must recognize that it is not an elusive entity to chase after but an abundant flow that is ever-present in the universe. When you operate from a place of scarcity, you inadvertently block the flow of money into your life. Instead, adopt an abundance mindset, understanding that the universe is infinitely abundant, and there is more than enough wealth for everyone. Trust that as you align your thoughts, feelings, and actions with abundance, money will naturally be drawn to you.

Embrace the concept of giving and receiving in equal measure. The more you give, the more you open yourself up to receiving. By giving generously and with an open heart, you create space for money to flow effortlessly into your life. Let go of any guilt or fear associated with money and replace it with gratitude and joy. Celebrate your financial wins, no matter how small, and express gratitude for the abundance that surrounds you.

Empowering Yourself for Abundance

To succeed in attracting and sustaining abundance, empower yourself with knowledge and understanding. Educate yourself on financial matters, seek advice from experts, and stay informed about investment opportunities. Knowledge is a powerful tool that empowers you to make informed decisions and take control of your financial destiny.

Furthermore, be conscious of the company you keep. Surround yourself with individuals who uplift and inspire you to grow financially. Engage in conversations about money with positivity and openness. Share your aspirations and challenges with like-minded individuals who can offer support and encouragement on your journey.

Transforming Challenges into Opportunities

As you continue on your path to financial success, remember that challenges are not roadblocks but stepping stones. Embrace setbacks as valuable learning experiences and opportunities for growth. Every obstacle you encounter is an opportunity to refine your money mindset, strengthen your resilience, and realign with your goals. Rather than being discouraged, view challenges as a necessary part of your journey to greatness.

Your Abundance is Your Responsibility

Remember, your abundance is not dependent on external circumstances; it is your responsibility to cultivate it from within. Take ownership of your financial decisions and their consequences. Empower yourself to make choices that align with your goals and values. Accept that you have the power to shape your financial future and that you are worthy of success and prosperity.

Continuing the Journey of Abundance

As we conclude this book, I encourage you to keep the flame of abundance burning bright within you. Embrace money as your best friend and partner in your journey through life. Cultivate a deep appreciation for the wealth that flows into your life and the opportunities it presents. Continue to educate yourself, seek growth, and be open to giving and receiving with a grateful heart.

As you navigate the highs and lows of your financial journey, remember that true abundance goes beyond monetary wealth. It encompasses joy, fulfillment, and making a positive impact on the lives of others. Embrace a holistic approach to abundance that includes nurturing your well-being, cultivating meaningful relationships, and leaving a legacy of positivity for future generations.

Your Success in Abundance Awaits

The keys to unlocking the secrets of money attraction and sustaining an abundant life are now in your hands. Armed with knowledge, a positive mindset, and a willingness to take action, you have the tools to transform your relationship with money and create a life of prosperity and purpose.

I am confident that your journey will be filled with successes, growth, and boundless opportunities. Trust in your ability to manifest your desires, and embrace every step of the way with gratitude and joy. As you embark on this new chapter of your life, remember that the universe is conspiring to support your dreams.

Thank you for joining me on this incredible journey of self-discovery and empowerment. May you be forever best friends with money, and may abundance flow abundantly in every aspect of your life. Here's to your prosperous and fulfilling future!

Keep shining bright, my friend.

With heartfelt wishes,

www.ingramcontent.com/pod-product-compliance
Lightning Source LLC
Chambersburg PA
CBHW071604270726

48661CB00018B/1164